The Essential Poets

❖❖

*BOOK/CASSETTE PACKAGES AVAILABLE

The Essential Clare

❖❖

John Clare

BORN   13 **JULY** 1793
DIED   20 **MAY** 1864

The Essential ❖
CLARE

Selected and with an
Introduction by
CAROLYN KIZER

The Ecco Press

The Ecco Press
100 West Broad Street
Hopewell, NJ 08525
Published simultaneously in Canada by
Penguin Books Canada Ltd., Ontario
Printed in the United States of America
Design by Reg Perry
First Edition

Library of Congress Cataloging-in-Publication Data
Clare, John, 1793–1864.
[Poems. Selections]
The essential Clare / selected and with an introduction by Carolyn
Kizer.—1st ed.
p. cm.—(The Essential poets; v. 16)
Includes bibliographical references.
$8.00
I. Kizer, Carolyn. II. Title. III. Series: Essential poets; v. 16.
PR4453.C6A6   1992
821'.7—dc20   92-10666 CIP
ISBN 0-88001-157-2

Portrait of John Clare by William Hilton
Courtesy of the National Portrait Gallery, London.

Contents

❖

SOURCES   111

ABOUT THE EDITOR   115

Acknowledgment

❖❖

The copyright of the Clare manuscript is owned by Eric Robinson. My thanks to him, and also to The John Clare Society and its publication, *The Journal of the John Clare Society*.

The Essential Clare

❖❖

Introduction

❖❖

John Clare is without doubt the most neglected great poet in our language. He was cursed with bad luck from the start. His first misfortune was to be born in 1793, five years after Byron, a year later than Shelley, and two years before Keats. (He was to outlive them all by many years and continued to write prolifically until the time of Browning and Tennyson, dying a year before the birth of Yeats.) Born earlier or later, he might have emerged from that group of eminent poets who achieved popular success. As it was, Clare experienced a brief flare of fame when his first book was published and then sank back into the obscurity that persisted until recent times.

What initially intrigued the British public was that Clare was published and publicized as "The Peasant Poet" and treated with the condescension accorded Robert Bloomfield and Stephen Duck, though Clare was no peasant but a landless laborer like his father. Clare contributed to this false stereotype with such self-deprecating references to his poems as "the unpolished heartfelt feelings of a lowly Clown" (a rustic) "who is not acquainted with the craft and Subtlety of Art to make them agreeable to the tasteful Eye."

In truth, Clare was exceptionally well-read: although he read everything he could get his hands on, from *Little Red Riding Hood* to *Pilgrim's Progress,* he also read and reread the prophetical books of the *Bible;* his shelves contained books on land surveying, botany, philosophy, astrology, and herbal medicine. In poetry, Thompson's *The Seasons* was an early favorite and a continuing influence—and probably the first book he ever bought, with painfully saved pennies. Clare knew the sonnets of Shakespeare, Milton, Dryden, and Surrey. He esteemed Pope at a time when that poet was out of fashion (a taste he shared with Byron); he was interested in Donne, who was in virtual eclipse then, and for a century to come.

In a letter to his publishers in October 1824, Clare wrote: "I never take up Johnson's *Lives* but I regret his beginning at the wrong end first and leaving out those beautiful minstrels of Elizabeth—had he forgot that there had been such poets as Spenser, Drayton, Suckling? But it was the booksellers' judgment that employed his pen and we know by experience most of their judgments lye in their pockets; so the poets of Elizabeth are still left in cobwebs and mystery." So speaks one "not acquainted with the craft and Subtlety of Art."

The worst curse laid on this physically fragile man was unremitting poverty and hard labor in the fields, fens, and quarries. Even at the height of his fame, when his first book sold four thousand copies in the first year (while Keats and Shelley sold barely five hundred copies each), his publishers paid him almost nothing, and he was forced to continue working as a common laborer. This work, and the unceasing anxiety he felt about keeping his parents, his wife, and his seven children from starvation, undoubtedly contributed to the mental illness that confined him to insane asylums for more than a quarter of a century, until his long life ended.

Clare was born in the Northamptonshire village of Helpston, which consisted of little more than a single street lined with cottages, taverns, and a church. The fens that lay to the north and east were a source of the "fen ague," a type of malaria for which the standard specifics were opium and brandy. Clare suffered from fen ague, and perhaps from the remedies as well, until he was put away. To the west and south of the village was a landscape with "a wealth of wild-flowers, woodlands, heaths and gentle valleys," where the birds were song-birds "rather than the coarse-voiced creatures of marsh and flood" as Edward Storey describes it in his life of Clare.

He was the eldest child of Parker and Anne Clare (his twin, a girl, died a few weeks after birth). His illiterate mother wanted him to have the best education the family could manage, in hopes that he would rise above the level of a field laborer. Clare went to a Dame's school in Helpston, for three months out of the year at most, as even little children were needed for tasks at home. Later he attended a village school in Glinton, two miles away, where the master was impressed with his reading and his remarkable memory. There he met a little girl named Mary Joyce, the daughter of a prosperous farmer. Mary was about eight when they met, Clare four years older. They parted in their teens, perhaps because Mary was above him socially, or perhaps because of Clare's shyness and reticence.

But Clare never forgot her, though he was to take a casual or romantic interest in many women. Mary was his muse for the rest of his life. The dozens upon dozens of poems he wrote to her—or wrote to other women in the days of his madness with Mary in mind—vary wildly in quality but attest to his never-fading adoration. Clare wrote that other Marys "excited my admiration, and the first creator of my warm passions was lost in a perplexed multitude of names."

Clare's formal education ended when he was thirteen so that he could hire out as a laborer like the other village boys, although he attended night school for a time. But his poet's education was not confined to book learning at school and book reading at home. His parents amused themselves in the evenings by singing the old folk ballads. Both parents were admired locally as tellers of tales; his father was a popular entertainer at village festivities and boasted that he knew more than a hundred traditional songs by heart.

A crone named Granny Bains taught him more ballads and narrative verses while he was tending sheep or scaring off crows. Clare loved to haunt the camp of the gypsies—"a quiet, pilfering, unprotected race" he was to write much later—to listen to their fiddles and learn their songs. One critic has said that the gypsies "had a strange fascination for Clare." Not so strange: while Clare and his kind joined "catchwork gangs," worked as plowboys, limeburners, and gardeners—unremitting labor—the gypsies were free.

Clare's songs were born in music, in the words of the great Clare scholar, Eric Robinson, "in the scrape of the fiddle and in the voices of his mother and father singing in that small cottage in Helpston." By his early teens he was composing ballads and rhymes in imitation of the models he had learned. He tried them out on his parents, who saw little merit in them and laughed, until Clare pretended he had copied them from a book. Then they approved.

Finding suitable surfaces on which to write was a problem then and for the rest of his life. At that time he used bits of bills on blue paper and brown wrapping paper from the grocer, and hid the poems in a hole in the wall. His mother, thinking he was merely practicing his handwriting, often used them as squibs for lighting the fire.

At one point, Clare was hired by the proprietor of the Blue Bell, a tavern where he worked for nearly a year, and where he learned to drink. His fits and starts of employment went on for years, but to detail them contributes little to understanding his development as a poet. His true occupation was to wander the woods and fields, lying silent in the grass for hours on end, inspecting the busy insects, admiring the weeds, or keeping watch over a bird's nest, carefully noting the color and number of its eggs while awaiting the parent bird's return. These are the themes in his poems that contemporary poets, if they are fortunate enough to know Clare's work, love the best.

Why is this? Clare's way of seeing and writing presaged a shift in sensibility that has only become fully accepted by poets of our own day. Unsophisticated though he seemed in London literary circles, with his funny grass-green coat, his uncouth table manners, and the comportment of a bumpkin, Clare was a sophisticated writer, a modern in a way that the others were not, with a sturdy trust in his own way of writing. Charles Lamb urged him to abandon natural speech and provincial phrasing: "I think you are too profuse with them. There is a rustick Cockneyism as little pleasing as ours of London. Transplant Arcadia to Helpstone." Clare didn't.

John Taylor, publisher of both Keats and Clare, advised him that "your Poetry is much the best when you are not describing common things, and if you would raise your Views generally, & speak of the Appearances of Nature . . . more philosophically (if I may say so) or with more Excitement, you would greatly improve these little poems." Clare wouldn't.

Earlier, Taylor wrote Clare that he thought Keats "wishes to say to you that your Images from Nature are too much introduced without being called for by a particular Sentiment." Clare was not about to take this lying down. Keats, he wrote, "keeps up a constant allusion or illusion to the Grecian mythology & there I cannot follow . . . the frequency of such classical accompaniments make it wearisome to the reader where behind every rose bush he looks for a Venus & under every laurel a thrumming Apollo." Nature, many of his critics and fellow poets felt, was to be used to illustrate ideas or philosophic concepts. Clare preferred to have Nature use *him,* to be the vessel through which the beauties and bounties of Nature would be poured out for all the world to know. "No ideas but in things"—as long as those "things" sang, squeaked, blossomed, nested, soared, or loved—would have been a motto quite acceptable to Clare.

Critics as recent as Edmund Gosse (1921) were fatigued by Clare's obsessive counting of bird's eggs and his careful description of their exact tint; repetition they regarded as simple carelessness was a conscious part of Clare's technique—what Gosse labeled "his redundant flow of verses." Clare composed hastily, but this was due to his compelling need to catch the experience in words even as it was unfolding for him. The specificity and particularity of his descriptions were an intrinsic part of his success in capturing immediate reality. (He fought to retain his dialect words because they conveyed his exact meaning; no word in the conventional literary vocabulary would do.) One sonnet that expresses this immediacy—Clare composing the poem as he walks along—is "Sudden Shower":

> Black grows the southern sky betokening rain
> And humming hive-bees homeward hurry by
> They feel the change so let us shun the grain
> And take the broad road while our feet are dry
> Ay there some dropples moistened on my face
> And pattered on my hat—tis coming nigh!
> Lets look about and find a sheltering place
> The little things around like you and I
> Are hurrying through the grass to shun the shower
> Here stoops an ash-tree—hark! the wind gets high
> But never mind, this ivy for an hour
> Rain as it may will keep us dryly here
> That little wren knows well his sheltering bower
> Nor leaves his dry house though we come so near.

One can picture Clare tucking a rain-spotted scrap of paper into his hat as he sheltered in the bower with the wren.

It is this immediacy, this absence of abstraction in favor of the real thing, which so attracts the contemporary reader and writer. Perhaps the modern sensibility is more ready to relish the bird poems with their close descriptions—counting the eggs!—where earlier commentators complained these poems were not poetry, but leaves from a naturalist's notebook. No critic has made that complaint about Theodore Roethke, who adored Clare and taught what was known of his poetry before the 1960s to so many of his students, including this one. One of his editors defined Clare's style as a composition of "frugality of epithet, vigor, and originality of verbs": verbs, the armature of the poem around which all else is molded! Apart from his natural proclivities, Clare must have learned from the Metaphysicals he loved, as Roethke learned from "the poets of Elizabeth" and Clare himself.

Theodore Roethke's line, "I'm odd and full of love," is a description that suits Clare even more accurately than it suits its author. Though the world of nature was Clare's constant theme, he lived equally in a world of love. Poem after poem contains the phrase, "I love to see" or "I love to hear"; poems begin with lines such as "I love thy shade / Wild arbour on the rude heath growing," or "I love in summer time to seek a seat / Wading the long grass where a path neer led / Patting their downy tops with idle feet," or "I love to drop in summer on the grass / & with unwearied eye mark pleasing things," or "I love to peep out on a summers morn / Just as the scouting rabbit seeks her shed," or "I love to roam in spring by hedgerow sides / These old enclosures mossed with many years . . ."

But then there is a variation: "I love thee sweet mary but love thee in fear . . ."

Mary, "whose heart was tender as a bird's," whose sensitive response to nature chimed so harmoniously with his own, was becoming the chief figure in his mental landscape, a half of him that made him whole:

> *We loved and in each others power felt nothing to condemn*
> *I was the leaf and she the flower And both grew on one stem . . .*

But the outer landscape of Clare's life was changing, and the change had begun before he was born. The infamous Enclosure Acts of Parliament were depriving cottagers and laborers of rights that had been theirs since the thirteenth century. Since the second quarter of the eighteenth century more than six million acres of land were appropriated by the great lords and other landholders for their own use. Eric Robinson says that Clare saw "venerable trees cut down, whole coppices destroyed, and the streams diverted from their natural courses. The commons were fenced off and 'No Trespassing' notices posted, old women were forbidden to gather sticks from the hedges, and laborers were transported for taking a hare for the pot." In an irony not lost on Clare, the laborer not only lost access to the land he had once freely roamed, but he had to drain, level, and fence it in the service of those who had stolen it from him:

> *But sweating slaves I do not blame*
> *Those slaves by wealth decreed*
> *No I should hurt their harmless name*
> *To brand 'em wi' the deed*
> *Although their aching hands did wield*
> *The axe that gave the blow*
> *Yet t'was not them that own'd the field*
> *Nor planned its overthrow . . .*

Some critics have said that had this poem been printed in full, Clare would have been labeled a radical. But the bulk of Clare's work announces that he was profoundly conservative in the old, true meaning since corrupted by our own politicians. His deepest desire was that the ways of nature and the ancient tracks of man and beast be left as they had always been.

In the winter of 1821, the owner of Clare's cottage threatened to chop down two ancient elms. Clare wrote to John Taylor:

> My two favorite elm trees at the back of the hut are condemned to die—it shocks me to relate but 'tis true. The savage who owns them thinks they have done their best and now he wants to make use of the benefits he can get from selling them. O was this country Egypt and I was but a Caliph the owner should lose his ears for his arrogant presumption and the first wretch that buried his axe in their roots should hang on their branches. . . . Yet this mourning over trees is all foolishness. A second thought tells me I am a fool; were people all to feel as I do the world could not be carried on—a green would not be ploughed up—a tree or bush would not be cut for firing or furniture, and everything they found when boys would remain in that state until they died.

Later, when Taylor asked a friend, Octavius Gilchrist, to intervene, Clare had third thoughts: "Let them die like the rest of us."

John Taylor was a bookseller who also discovered and printed Keats. Clare's attempts to find someone to print his work met with repeated rebuffs and frustrations. Finally, in 1819, he showed his manuscript to a Stamford bookseller named Drury, who sent it to Taylor, his cousin. Taylor and his partner, Hessey, were interested, and after extensively editing Clare's spelling and excising passages thought to offend the delicate-minded public, they published *Poems*

Descriptive of Rural Life and Scenery in 1820, which caused a mild sensation.

For a while, Clare enjoyed his little fame: he went to London and was entertained by Taylor's acquaintances, among them Charles Lamb, George Darley, H. F. Cary (the translator of Dante), William Hazlitt, Samuel Taylor Coleridge, and Thomas De Quincey. (Clare's assessment of these gentlemen makes amusing reading. His descriptions and estimations of each man's character are acute and perceptive and not often unkind, only so when their condescensions and suggestions for his improvement were unwelcome.) For his first London visit, Clare showed up in a coat of grass green, which caused some comment. Thomas Hood wrote that the coat was "shining verdantly out from the grave-coloured suits of the literati." Several critics have remarked on the appropriate symbolism of the coat, dubbing Clare "the green man."

Only two months after the publication of *Poems Descriptive,* Clare married Patty Turner, who was seven months pregnant. Clare, like Blake, married an illiterate woman who signed her name on the marriage certificate with a crude "X." Their daughter, Anne Maria, was born on June 2, 1820:

> *& much I wish what ere may be*
> *The lot my child that falls to thee*
> *Nature neer may let thee see*
> *   Her glass betimes*
> *But keep thee from my failings free*
> *   Nor itch at rhymes . . .*
>
> *May thou unknown to rhyming bother*
> *Be ignorant as is thy mother*
> *& in thy manners such another*
> *   Save sins nigh guest*

> *And then wi scaping this & tother*
> *Thou mayst be blest . . .*

These stanzas from "To An Infant Daughter" may reveal Clare's ambivalence about Patty, ignorant and gentle, and also about himself. The "glass" is a mirror of nature; but associated as it is with "failings" (in the following line) it could also refer, consciously or otherwise, to Clare's drinking, which had become a problem.

It's no wonder he increasingly sought refuge with rough companions at the Blue Bell. Child followed child in rapid succession, and he had his parents to support as well. He worried constantly about how he would feed them and compared his situation with that of Bloomfield, who "had not a hundred pounds a year to maintain 5 or 6 in the family why I have not fifty pounds to maintain 8 with. This is a hungry difference."

Also, his was a mind that overflowed "with excess of joys that spring from solitude," that treasured introspection and "speaking silence," and he was confined to a tiny cottage swarming with little children and subject to the ceaseless stream of words from a voluble wife. By the fall of 1823 Clare had become terribly depressed. His children were frail and sickly, he suffered from fen ague, he was deeply in debt. And he thought that he had fallen in love again. Yet he continued to write exquisite poems, many of which remained unpublished for a hundred years. Poems such as "The Nightmare" and "The Dream," which reveal his troubled mind—the latter containing a line worthy of Marvell: "When Time in terror drops his draining glass / And all things mortal, like to shadows, pass." Poems of fragile beauty like "Evening Primrose": "Almost as pale as moonbeams are / or its companionable star."

And at the opposite extreme, romping ballads like "The Toper's Rant":

> *Give me an old crone of a fellow*
> > *Who loves to drink ale in a horn*
> *And sing racy songs when hes mellow*
> > *Which topers sang ere he was born*
> *For such a friend fate should be thankéd*
> > *And line but our pockets with brass*
> *We'd sooner suck ale through a blanket*
> > *Than thimbles of wine through a glass . . .*

Then there is the final couplet of "Spring Morning," which sums up Clare as well as any lines he ever wrote: "The flowers join lips below; the leaves above, / And every sound that meets the ear is Love."

After protracted negotiations and pressing letters from Clare, who had become more adamant about changes in his language, his *The Village Minstrel* was published in two volumes late in 1821. The book sold a respectable eight hundred copies, but the critics' interest had cooled. The "peasant poet" had gone out of fashion. As usual he was paid almost nothing by his negligent, or callous, publisher. Clare's third book, *The Shepherd's Calendar,* came out in 1827. Taylor had become more severe about eliminating dialect words and entire passages that he feared might offend Clare's proper "patrons." Clare, desperate to be published, consented, though not without lasting resentment.

Two years earlier, Clare noted in his diary a dream which proved prophetic:

> I had a very odd dream last night and I take it as an ill omen, for I don't expect that the book will meet with a better fate. I thought I had one of the proofs of the new poems from London, and after looking at it awhile it shrank through my hands like sand, crumbling into dust.

Indeed, the book was a failure, selling but four hundred copies in two years. Taylor made what proved to be a devastating suggestion: Clare should take over the remaining copies and sell them from door to door in the environs of Helpston. Clare was snubbed at every turn, particularly by those eager to humiliate one who had got "above his station." Frantic for money, Clare turned to writing sentimental or patriotic verses for popular annuals of the day with titles like *Friendship's Offering*. But more often than not, these journals failed to pay him.

Farmers in his own neighborhood refused to hire him as a laborer. He was regarded as eccentric (as he had been since childhood), possibly simpleminded, muttering aloud as he wandered, perhaps a poacher, perhaps, indeed, mad. He drank too much, hung out with gypsies and other coarse companions, and was too fond of women. Helpston never forgave his first success. "I live here among the ignorant like a lost man."

At this dark hour Clare and his family were offered a cottage three miles from Helpston at Northborough. Some of Clare's finest poetry resulted from what was, for him, a traumatic change of environment. Many scholars have found his extreme sense of dislocation puzzling. Although the new place was considerably larger, suited to the needs of his growing family, there were important differences in the two locations. The poem "Decay" tells some of the story. In the following line, "I often think that west is gone," one sees Clare has misplaced even his sense of direction:

> Love's sun went down without a frown
> For very joy it used to grieve us
> I often think that west is gone
> Ah cruel time to undecieve us
> The stream it is a naked stream
> Where we on sundays used to ramble

The sky hangs oer a broken dream
The brambles nothing but a bramble
O poesy is on its wane
I cannot find her haunts again . . .

Yet the poems kept coming. He found the coins to buy a new notebook for a collection he wanted to call *A Midsummer Cushion*—named for a piece of turf covered with wildflowers with which his countrymen and women decorated their cottages. A kindly, intrusive, proper-minded patroness, a Mrs. Emmerson, insisted the collection be called by the pedestrian title *The Rural Muse*. It was published in 1835, sold poorly, and attracted very little attention.

Clare's life, always precarious, was falling apart. His mother died, and his father lived with the Clares and their seven children. Clare showed increasing signs of mental instability, including his obsession with Mary Joyce: he believed that she was his first wife and Patty his second. This cannot have contributed to harmony around the hearthside. (Mary Joyce was living, unmarried, just three miles away, but it is not thought that she and Clare had had any contact for many years.)

In 1837 Clare was committed to High Beach Asylum, in the charge of Dr. Matthew Allen, an unusually sympathetic and progressive physician. Even so, Clare ran away from High Beach in 1841. He left an extraordinary account of this three-day journey, during which he had nothing to eat but a handful of grass and a half-pint of beer given him by a stranger on horseback. By the end of this painful odyssey, published as "Journey out of Essex," Clare says that he was met by a cart with a man and a woman and a boy in it; "the woman jumped out and caught fast hold of my hands and wished me to get into the cart but I refused and thought her either drunk or mad but when I was told it was my second wife Patty I got in and was soon at Northborough . . . but Mary was not there." Clare was then nearly forty-eight years old.

Patty hoped to keep him at home, as he was no danger to anyone, but this proved impossible. He went back to High Beach for a few months longer, and then was committed to the Northampton County Asylum, where he remained until he died at age seventy. A wonderfully sensitive description of Clare by Cyrus Redding, a visitor to High Beach in 1841, was applicable to Clare's state for the rest of his life: "The principal token of his mental eccentricity was the introduction of prize-fighting, in which he seemed to imagine he was to engage; but the allusion to it was made in the way of interpolation in the middle of the subject on which he was discoursing, brought in abruptly, and abandoned with equal suddenness . . . as if the machinery of thought was dislocated, so that one part of it got off its pivot, and protruded into the regular workings; or *as if a note had got into a piece of music which had no business there.*" (Italics mine.)

Dr. Allen believed that, given proper care, Clare could recover, but local doctors thought they knew better, and one Dr. Skrimshaw condemned him to the madhouse with the now infamous phrase, "After years addicted to poetical prosings." This, fortunately for posterity, was an addiction that nothing could cure. Although he might have lived more contentedly at home, given enough to eat and the assurance of minimum economic security, it is hard to believe Clare's slippery hold on his identity could have been annealed. The poems tell us this more powerfully than the numerous descriptions of Clare's conviction that at various times he was Shakespeare, Lord Byron, or a noted prizefighter of the day:

> *Say maiden wilt thou go with me*
> *Through this sad non-identity*

> *Where parents live and are forgot*
> *And sisters live and know us not . . .*

> *At once to be, and not to be*
> *That was, and is not—yet to see*
> *Things pass Like shadows—and the sky*
> *Above, below, around us lie . . .*

Or those most famous lines of his:

> *I am—yet what I am, none cares or knows;*
>   *My friends forsake me like a memory lost:*
> *I am the self-consumer of my woes;*
>   *They rise and vanish in oblivion's host,*
> *Like shadows in love's frenzied stifled throes:*
> *And yet I am, and live—like vapours toss't*

> *Into the nothingness of scorn and noise . . .*

Some critics—notably Geoffrey Grigson, who edited *Poems of John Clare's Madness* in 1949—believe the poetry from this period constitutes Clare's greatest work. But despite poems of undoubted genius like "I Am" and "A Vision," most of the poems written during his incarceration lack the freshness, the immediacy of his vision, and the glorious specifics of his earlier work. Yet we would not be without them:

> *Are flowers the winter's choice*
> *Is love's bed always snow . . .*

I would trade the bulk of late nineteenth-century poetry for that one couplet. It has that quality, unique to Clare, which he describes in the first line of another very late poem, "I speak in low calm breathing whispers."

Clare was well treated in the house of his second sequestration. He was given a good deal of freedom, especially in the earlier years, when he was allowed to wander in the town, smoking his pipe and admiring pretty girls to whom he might write and dedicate a poem on the spot. He grew strong and healthy, having plenty to eat and excellent care. But the true hero of these years was the house-steward of the asylum, W. F. Knight. He admired Clare's poetry, copied it out, and saved it. Many poems survive only because of the transcriptions he made. Many, many are the poems to Mary, at first a human girl, then a Muse, then something like a Saint, at last a Goddess, the presiding deity of his life:

> I sleep with thee and wake with thee
> And yet thou art not there:—
> I fill my arms, with thoughts of thee,
> And press the common air . . .

Read the poem which begins, "Black absence hides upon the past . . ."

All the same, Clare was a prisoner, more closely held as the years went on, under a stricter management. And he knew where he was, in "the land of Sodom where all the people's brains are turned the wrong way." And he was unbearably lonely. One would like to believe that somewhere his soul may know of the devoted friends he is making these days, two hundred years after his birth.

—CAROLYN KIZER

Note

As must be recognized by now, this Essential series is edited exclusively by poets—poets who have a lifelong affection for and knowledge of the poet they have selected. Our choices are, therefore, more personal than those of scholars and academics who feel the need to represent the entire scope of the work. I have omitted many long and important poems vital to the understanding of Clare's attitude toward his milieu and his criticisms of society as he saw it. This is partly to compensate for the emphasis of many critics, some of them gifted Marxists, on a sociological approach to Clare that neglects his primary concern: the destruction of the countryside that he loved. One wishes that social historians would make more use of these poems and literary critics less. I have focused, in my choices, on the prosody, believing with all my heart that Clare was not just a poet born but a skilled craftsman who knew what he was doing.

As I mention in the Introduction, Clare wrote many poems and ballads for popular albums of a sentimental and patriotic bent. Clare's late poems in Scots dialect are largely worthless—and the verses on patriotic military themes almost entirely so. It's wonderful how the ruling classes have habitually debased the poor, and yet other working-class poets besides Clare can always be counted upon to arise and spout patriotic platitudes.

Throughout, I have omitted poems which rely on conventional epithets—snowy bosoms, ruby lips, and the like—and poems, admired by many, which are mechanically stressed.

Beyond these strictures, it has pained me more than I can say to have to leave out so many beautiful poems. I can only refer the interested reader to The Oxford Authors *John Clare* (1984) edited by Eric Robinson and David Powell.

—C. K.

I. Animals, Primroses, Bees, and Ivy

◆◆

*For my part I love to look on nature with a poetic feeling which magnifys the pleasure . . .
I love to see the nightingale in its hazel retreat and the cuckoo hiding in its solitudes of oaken
foliage and not to examine their carcasses in glass cases . . . well everyone to his hobby I have
none of this curiosity about me tho I feel as happy as they can in finding a new species of field
flower or butter flye which I had not seen before yet I have no desire further to dry the plant
or turture Butterflye by sticking it on a coark board with a pin. . . .*

—Clare

Sheep in Winter

The sheep get up and make their many tracks
And bear a load of snow upon their backs
And gnaw the frozen turnip to the ground
With sharp quick bite, and then go noising round
The boy that pecks the turnips all the day
And knocks his hands to keep the cold away
And laps his legs in straw to keep them warm
And hides behind the hedges from the storm
The sheep, as tame as dogs, go where he goes
And try to shake their fleeces from the snows
Then leave their frozen meal and wander round
The stubble stack that stands beside the ground
And lie all night and face the drizzling storm
And shun the hovel where they might be warm

Mouse's Nest

I found a ball of grass among the hay
And progged it as I passed and went away   *prodded*
And when I looked I fancied something stirred
And turned again and hoped to catch the bird
When out an old mouse bolted in the wheats
With all her young ones hanging at her teats
She looked so odd and so grotesque to me
I ran and wondered what the thing could be
And pushed the knapweed bunches where I stood
When the mouse hurried from the craking brood
The young ones squeaked, and as I went away
She found her nest again among the hay
The water o'er the pebbles scarce could run
And broad old cesspools glittered in the sun

The Badger

The badger grunting on his woodland track
With shaggy hide and sharp nose scrowed   *scratched*, or *scored*
    with black
Roots in the bushes and the woods and makes
A great huge burrow in the ferns and brakes
With nose on ground he runs an awkward pace
And anything will beat him in the race
The shepherd's dog will run him to his den
Followed and hooted by the dogs and men
The woodman when the hunting comes about
Go round at night to stop the foxes out
And hurrying through the bushes ferns and brakes

Nor sees the many holes the badger makes
And often through the bushes to the chin
Breaks the old holes and tumbles headlong in

When midnight comes a host of dogs and men
Go out and track the badger to his den
And put a sack within the hole and lie
Till the old grunting badger passes by
He comes and hears they let the strongest loose
The old fox hears the noise and drops the goose
The poacher shoots and hurries from the cry
And the old hare half wounded buzzes by.
They get a forkèd stick to bear him down
And clap the dogs and take him to the town   *set the dogs on*
And bait him all the day with many dogs
And laugh and shout and fright the scampering hogs
He runs along and bites at all he meets;
They shout and hollo down the noisy streets

He turns about to face the loud uproar
And drives the rebels to their very doors
The frequent stone is hurled where'ere they go
When badgers fight, then everyone's a foe
The dogs are clapt and urged to join the fray
The badger turns and drives them all away
Though scarcely half as big, dimute and small   *diminutive*
He fights with dogs for hours and beats them all
The heavy mastiff savage in the fray
Lies down and licks his feet and turns away
The bulldog knows his match and waxes cold
The badger grins and never leaves his hold
He drives the crowd and follows at their heels
And bites them through—the drunkard swears and reels

The frightened women take the boys away
The blackguard laughs and hurries on the fray
He tries to reach the woods an awkward race
But sticks and cudgels quickly stop the chase
He turns again and drives the noisy crowd
And beats the many dogs in noises loud
He drives away and beats them every one
And then they loose them all and set them on
He falls as dead and kicked by boys and men
Then starts and grins and drives the crowd again
Till kicked and torn and beaten out he lies
And leaves his hold and cackles, groans and dies.

The Primrose Bank

'Tis Spring: day roams with flowers
    Down every little lane
  And the night is hardly night
But a round of happy hours

Yes, night is happy night
    The sky is full of stars,
  Like worlds in peace they lie
Enjoying one delight

The dew is on the thorn
    And the primrose underneath
  Just against the mossy root
Is smiling to the morn

With its little brimming eye
    And its yellow rims so pale
  And its crimp and curdled leaf—
Who can pass its beauties by

Without a look of love
When we tread the little path
That skirts the woodland ride?
Who can pass nor look above

To Him who blesses earth
With these messengers of spring
And decorates the fields
For our happiness and mirth?

I cannot: for I go
In my fancy once again
In the woods and little holts
Where the primrose used to grow

The woodbank seemed so fair
And the hedgerow in the lane
Seemed so sweet that scores of times
Have I wished my cottage there

And felt that lovely mood
As a birthright God had given
To muse in the green wood
And meet the smiles of heaven

And though no culture comes
To the places where they grow
Every spring finds more and more
Till the wood's all yellow blooms

The woodman's guessing way
Oft tramples many down
But there's not a blossom missing
When he comes another day

The woods have happy guests
              And the birds sing twice as loud
        When they meet such crowds of blossoms
Underneath their little nests

As beauties for the spring
              Their maker sends them forth
        That man may have his mirth
And nature laugh and sing

For when roaming where they flower
              They seemed to make woods happy
        And amid the green light round them
I've spent many a happy hour

But since I used to stray
              In their hazel haunts for joy
        The world has found the happy spots
And took the charm away

It has tracked the pleasant springs
              Like armies on their march
        Till dearest spots that used to be
Are naught but common things

Save that their sights employ
              Balm gales and sunny blooms
        The mind in shaping heavens
As one continued joy

Hares at Play

The birds are gone to bed, the cows are still
And sheep lie panting on each old mole-hill
And underneath the willow's grey-green bough
Like toil a-resting—lies the fallow plough
The timid hares throw daylight fears away
On the lane's road to dust and dance and play
Then dabble in the grain by naught deterred
To lick the dew-fall from the barley's beard
Then out they start again and round the hill
Like happy thoughts—dance—squat—and loiter still
Till milking maidens in the early morn
Jingle their yokes and sturt them in the corn;   *start*
Through well-known beaten paths each nimbling hare
Sturts quick as fear—and seeks its hidden lair

Wild Bees

These children of the sun which summer brings
As pastoral minstrels in her merry train
Pipe rustic ballads upon busy wings
And glad the cotters' quiet toils again   *cottage dwellers*
The white-nosed bee that bores its little hole
In mortared walls and pipes its symphonies
And never absent couzen, black as coal   *cousin*
That Indian-like, bepaints its little thighs
With white and red bedight for holiday
Right earlily a-morn do pipe and play
And with their legs stroke slumber from their eyes
And aye so fond they of their singing seem
That in their holes abed at close of day

They still keep piping in their honey dreams
And larger ones that thrum on ruder pipe
Round the sweet smelling closen and rich woods   *small fields*
Where tawny white and red flush clover buds
Shine bonnily and bean fields blossom ripe
Shed dainty perfumes and give honey food
To those sweet poets of the summer fields
Me much delighting as I stroll along
The narrow path that hay-laid meadow yields
Catching the windings of their wandering song
The black and yellow bumble first on wing
To buzz among the sallow's early flowers   *willow's*
Hiding its nest in holes from fickle spring
Who stints his rambles with her frequent showers,
And one that may for wiser piper pass
In livery dress half sables and half red
Who laps a moss ball in the meadow grass
And hoards her stores when April showers have fled;
And russet commoner who knows the face
Of every blossom that the meadow brings
Starting the traveller to a quicker pace
By threatening round his head in many rings
These sweeten summer in their happy glee
By giving for her honey melody

Young Lambs

The spring is coming by a many signs
    The trays are up, the hedges broken down
That fenced the haystack, and the remnant shines
    Like some old antique fragment weathered brown
And where suns peep, in every sheltered place
    The little early buttercups unfold

A glittering star or two—till many trace
   The edges of the blackthorn clumps in gold
And then a little lamb bolts up behind
   The hill and wags his tail to meet the yoe   *ewe*
And then another, sheltered from the wind
   Lies all his length as dead—and lets me go
Close by and never stirs, but beaking lies   *basking*
   With legs stretched out as though he could not rise

To the Ivy

Dark creeping Ivy, with thy berries brown
   That fondly twists on ruins all thine own
Old spire-points studding with a leafy crown
   Which every minute threatens to dethrone
With fearful eye I view thy height sublime
   & oft with quicker step retreat from thence
Where thou in weak defiance strive with Time
   & hold his weapons in a dread suspense
But bloom of ruins thou art dear to me
   When far from danger's way thy gloomy pride
Wreathes picturesque around some ancient tree
   That bows his branches by some fountain-side
Then sweet it is from summer suns to be
With thy green darkness overshadowing me

The Hedgehog

The hedgehog hides beneath the rotten hedge
And makes a great round nest of grass and sedge
Or in a bush or in a hollow tree
And many often stoops and say they see

Him roll and fill his prickles full of crabs   *crab apples*
And creep away; and where the magpie dabs
His wing at muddy dyke in aged root
He makes a nest and fills it full of fruit
On the hedge bottom hunts for crabs and sloes
And whistles like a cricket as he goes
It rolls up like a ball a shapeless hog
When gypsies hunt it with their noisy dogs
I've seen it in their camps, they call it sweet
Though black and bitter and unsavoury meat

But they who hunt the fields for rotten meat
And wash in muddy dyke and call it sweet
And eat what dogs refuse where ere they dwell
Care little either for the taste or smell
They say they milk the cows and when they lie
Nibble their fleshy teats and make them dry
But they who've seen the small head like a hog
Rolled up to meet the savage of a dog
With mouth scarce big enough to hold a straw
Will ne'er believe what no one ever saw
But still they hunt the hedges all about
And shepherd dogs are trained to hunt them out
They hurl with savage force the stick and stone
And no one cares and still the strife goes on

The Lady-Fly

Tenant of leaves & flowers & glossy stalks
   The wild profusion that the summer brings
Hiding in crowding beans & benty
     baulks   *a strip of grass dividing fields*
    Where, on the knapweed while the cricket sings

I often watch thee prune thy speckled wings
On the smooth stem advancing yet more high
    Till with the help the puffing zephyr brings
Thou'lt stretch thy finer wings of gauze & fly
In changing scenes more snug & cool to lie
    Ah, when a cow-boy I at east reclined
Upon a thymy hill & thou wert nigh
    What fond inquiries filled my curious mind
How have I watched thy pastimes, lady-fly
    & thought thee happiest creature of thy kind

The Vixen

Among the taller wood with ivy hung
The old fox plays and dances round her young
She snuffs and barks if any passes by
And swings her tail and turns prepared to fly
The horseman hurries by, she bolts to see
And turns again from danger never free
If any stands she runs among the poles
And barks and snaps and drives them* in the holes
The shepherd sees them and the boy goes by
And gets a stick and progs the hole to try   *pokes*
They get all still and lie in safety sure
And out again when safety is secure
And start and snap at blackbirds bouncing by
To fight and catch the great white butterfly

*the young foxes

The Fox

The shepherd on his journey heard when nigh
His dog among the bushes barking high
The ploughman ran and gave a hearty shout
He found a weary fox and beat him out
The ploughman laughed and would have ploughed him in
But the old shepherd took him for the skin
He lay upon the furrow stretched and dead
The old dog lay and licked the wounds that bled
The ploughman beat him till his ribs would crack
And then the shepherd slung him at his back
And when he rested to his dog's surprise
The old fox started from his dead disguise
And while the dog lay panting in the sedge
He up and snapt and bolted through the hedge

He scampered to the bushes far away
The shepherd called the ploughman to the fray
The ploughman wished he had a gun to shoot
The old dog barked and followed the pursuit
The shepherd threw his hook and tottered past
The ploughman ran but none could go so fast
The woodman threw his faggot from the way
And ceased to chop and wondered at the fray
But when he saw the dog and heard the cry
He threw his hatchet but the fox was by
The shepherd broke his hook and lost the skin
He found a badger hole and bolted in
They tried to dig but safe from danger's way
He lived to chase the hounds another day

Evening Primrose

When once the sun sinks in the west
And dew-drops pearl the evening's breast
Almost as pale as moonbeams are
Or its companionable star
The evening primrose opes anew
Its delicate blossoms to the dew
And shunning hermit-like the light
Wastes its fair bloom upon the night
Who blindfold to its fond caresses
Knows not the beauty he possesses
Thus it blooms on till night is by
When day looks out with open eye
Abashed at the gaze it cannot shun
It faints and withers and is done

II. Helpston: Poems 1809–1831

❖❖

There once were lanes in nature's freedom dropt,
There once were paths that every valley wound—
Inclosure came, and every path was stopt;
Each tyrant fix'd his sign where paths were found,
To hint a trespass now who cross'd the ground:
Justice is made to speak as they command;
The high road now must be each stinted bound:
—Inclosure, thou'rt a curse upon the land.

                    —from "The Village Minstrel"

Noon

All how silent and how still
Nothing heard but yonder mill
While the dazzled eye surveys
All around a liquid blaze
And amid the scorching gleams
If we earnest look, it seems
As if crooked bits of glass
Seem'd repeatedly to pass
Oh! for a puffing breeze to blow
But breezes are all strangers now
Not a twig is seen to shake
Nor the smallest bent to quake

From the river's muddy side
Not a curve is seen to glide
And no longer on the stream
Watching lies the silver bream
Forcing, from repeated springs
'Verges in successive rings'*
Bees are faint, and cease to hum
Birds are overpower'd and dumb
And no more love's oaten strains
Sweetly through the air complains
Rural voices all are mute
Tuneless lies the pipe and flute
Shepherds, with their panting sheep
In the swaliest corner creep   *shadiest*
And from the tormenting heat
All are wishing to retreat
Huddled up in grass and flowers
Mowers wait for cooler hours
And the cow-boy seeks the sedge
Ramping in the woodland hedge
While his cattle o'er the vales
Scamper with uplifted tails
Others not so wild and mad
That can better bear the gad   *gadfly*
Underneath the hedgerow lunge
Or if nigh in waters plunge
Oh! to see how flowers are took
How it grieves me when I look
Ragged-robins, once so pink
Now are turn'd as black as ink
And the leaves, being scorched so much

*from Cunningham's 'Day'

Even crumble at the touch
Drowking lies the meadow-sweet   *drooping*
Flopping down beneath one's feet
While to all the flowers that blow
If in open air they grow
Th'injurious deed alike is done
By the hot relentless sun
E'en the dew is parched up
From the teasel's jointed cup
O poor birds! where must ye fly
Now your water-pots are dry
If ye stay upon the heath
Ye'll be chok'd and clamm'd to death   *starved*
Therefore leave the shadeless goss   *gorse*
Seek the spring-head lin'd with moss

There your little feet may stand
Safely printing on the sand
While, in full possession, where
Purling eddies ripple clear
You with ease and plenty blest
Sip the coolest and the best
Then away! and wet your throats
Cheer me with your warbling notes
'Twill not noon the more revive
While I wander to contrive
For myself a place as good
In the middle of a wood
There aside some mossy bank
Where the grass in bunches rank
Lifts its down on spindles high
Shall be where I'll choose to lie
Fearless of the things that creep

There I'll think, and there I'll sleep
Caring not to stir at all,
Till the dew begins to fall

A Reflection in Autumn

Now Autumn's come, adieu the pleasing greens
    The charming landscape, and the flow'ry plain
All have deserted from these motley scenes
    With blighted yellow ting'd, and russet stain

Though desolation seems to triumph here
    Yet this is Spring to what we still shall find
The trees must all in nakedness appear
    'Reft of their foliage by the blust'ry wind

Just so 'twill fare with me in Autumn's Life
    Just so I'd wish—but may the trunk and all
Die with the leaves—nor taste that wintry strife
    When sorrows urge—and fear impedes the fall

Impromptu on Winter

O winter, what a deadly foe
Art thou unto the mean and low
What thousands now half-pin'd and bare
Are forced to stand thy piercing air
All day, near numbed to death wi' cold
Some petty gentry to uphold
Paltry proudlings, hard as thee

Dead to all humanity—
Oh, the weather's cold and snow
Cutting winds that round me blow
But much more the killing scorn
Oh—the day that I was born
Friendless—poor as I can be
Struck wi' death o' poverty
But why need I the winter blame
To me all seasons come the same
Now winter bares each field and tree
She finds that trouble sav'd in me
Stript already—penniless!
Nothing boasting but distress
And when spring chill'd nature cheers
Still my old complaint she hears
Summer too, in plenty blest
Finds me poor, and still distrest
Kind autumn too, so liberal and so free
Brings my old well-known present—Poverty.

Stanzas from *Winter*

.　　.　　.

In winter's surly depth how sweet
To meet those comforts we desire
Possessing some snug corner seat
Where blazes nigh the welcome fire
Warming ones toes upon the hearth
And reading poems not too long
While basks the cat in burring mirth
While crickets sing their winter song.

And winter's tiresome hours to cheat
Have means to visit now and then
Where neighbors o'er their tankard meet
And there the corner share again
Each comfort suiting best to choose
To sit and crump warm penny rolls   *crunch*
Or take short snatches o'er the news
While warms the nappy on the coals.

And when suns creep the warmest height
And north winds whisper nearly still
When greening patches meet the sight
On southward slant of bank or hill
And berries freed from rime awhile
Shines red on hedgerow twigs again
One may a midday hour beguile
To walk in shielding wood and plain.

.   .   .

Each twig when touch'd though hardly stirr'd
Its white shower litters to the ground
And from the shake of startl'd bird
The rime-like powder puthers round   *puffs*
And as one fails those tracks to meet
By shepherds made, and foddering boys
The snow shrinks from our hast'ning feet,
Harsh crumping with incessant noise.

Now view the prospect where we will
On woods above or vales below
Or nigh or distant winter still
Stretches his dazzling scene of snow
The very spire-points catch the eye

As changed with winter's frowning pride
And where a sunbeam cannot lie
Shine whitened on their northern side.

.   .   .

Made bold by want in many a flock
The ringdoves fly from solitude
And mingling share with friendly stock
A portion of their winter food,
A meal which providence bestows
Where hardy turnip roots abound
And oft one sees upon the snows
Their little footprints dinted round.

.   .   .

But short is nature's waking hopes:
A frowning cloud may cross the skies
When sun and warmth and all elopes
And shrivelled leaf and daisy dies
A cuckoo's songs in summer cease
As swallows from the autumn flew
So flies in mystery winter's peace
And storms steal on to frown anew.

And give me then as now at eve
The chimney corner's idle joys
As day's cold scenes my rambles leave
To list the kettle's simmering noise
And while the chimney mocks the blast
And windows quake with jarring din
Let doors and shutters tightened fast
Keep cold night out and comfort in.

Approach of Spring

Sweet are the omens of approaching Spring,
    When gay the eldern sprouts her winged leaves,   *elder tree*
When tootling robins carol-welcomes sing,
    And sparrows chelp glad tidings from the eaves.   *chirp*
What lovely prospects wait each wakening hour,
    When each new day some novelty displays;
How sweet the sunbeam melts the crocus flower,
    Whose borrow'd pride shines dizen'd in his rays:
Sweet, new-laid hedges flush their tender greens;
Sweet peep the arum-leaves their shelter screens;
    Ah! sweet is all which I'm denied to share:
Want's painful hindrance sticks me to her stall—
    But still Hope's smiles unpoint the thorns of Care,
Since Heaven's eternal Spring is free for all.

Recollections after an Evening Walk

Just as the even bell rung we set out
To wander the fields & the meadows about
& the first thing we markt that was lovely to view
Was the sun hung on nothing & bidding adieu
He seemd like a ball of pure gold in the west
In a cloud like a mountain blue dropping to rest
The skies all around him were tingd wi his rays
& the trees at a distance seemd all on a blaze
Till lower & lower & sunk from our sight
& blue mist came creeping wi silence & night
The woodman then ceased wi his hatchet to hack
& bent away home wi his kid on his back
The mower too lapt up his sythe from our sight

& put on his jacket & bid us good night
The thresher once lumping we heard him no more   *threshing*
He left his barn dust & had shut up his door
The shepherd had told all his sheep in his pen
& humming his song sought his cottage agen
But the sweetest of all seeming music to me
Were the songs of the clumsy brown beetle & bee
The one was a hastning away to his hive
The other was just from his sleeping alive
& our hats he kept knocking as if hed no eyes
& when batted down he was puzzled to rise
The little gay moth too was lovely to view
A dancing with lily white wings in the dew
He wisked oer the water pudge flirting & airy   *puddle*
& perched on the down headed grass like a fairy
& there came the snail from his shell peeping out
As fearful & cautious as thieves on the rout
The sly jumping frog too had venturd to tramp
& the glow worm had just gun to light up his lamp
To sip of the dew the worm peepd from his den
But dreading our footsteps soon vanishd agen
& numbers of creatures appeard in our sight
That live in the silence & sweetness of night
Climbing up the tall grasses or scaling the bough
But these were all nameless unnoticd till now
& then we wound round neath the brooks willow row
& lookt at the clouds that kept passing below
The moons image too in the brook we could see't
As if twas the other world under our feet
& we listnd well pleased at the guggles & groans
The water made passing the pebbles & stones
& then we turned up by the rut rifted lane
& sought for our cot & the village again
For night gatherd round & shut all from the eye

& a black sultry cloud crept all over the sky
The dew on the bush soon as touchd it would drop
& the grass neath our feet was as wet as a mop
& as to the town we approachd very fast
The bat even popt in our face as he past
& the crickets sung loud as we went by the house
& by the barn side we saw many a mouse
Quirking round for the kernels that litterd about   *searching*
As shook from the straw which the thresher hurld out
& then we came up to our cottage once more
& shut out the night dew & lockt up the door
The dog barkd a welcome well pleasd at our sight
& the owl oer our cot flew & whoopt a good night

Stanzas from *Helpston Green*

Ye injur'd fields ye once were gay
When nature's hand display'd
Long waving rows of willows gray
And clumps of hawthorn shade
But now alas your hawthorn bowers
All desolate we see
The tyrant's hand their shade devours
And cuts down every tree

Not trees alone have felt their force
Whole woods beneath them bow'd
They stopt the winding runlet's course
And flowery pastures ploughed
To shrub nor tree throughout thy fields
They no compassion show
The uplifted axe no mercy yields
But strikes a fatal blow

The green's gone too—ah lovely scene
No more the king cup gay
Shall shine its yellow o'er the green
And add a golden ray
No more the herdsman's early call
Shall bring the cows to feed
No more the milkmaid's awkward brawl
Bright echo in the mead

Both milkmaid's shouts and herdsman's call
Have vanish'd with the green
The king cup's yellow shades and all
Shall never more be seen
For all the cropping that does grow
Will so efface the scene
That after times will hardly know
It ever was a green

. . .

The Wheat Ripening

What time the wheat field tinges rusty brown
And barley bleaches in its mellow grey
Tis sweet some smooth mown baulk to wander down
Or cross the fields on footpaths narrow way
Just in the mealey light of waking day
As glittering dewdrops moist the maiden's gown
And sparkling bounces from her nimble feet
Journying to milking from the neighbouring town
Making life bright with song—and it is sweet

To mark the grazing herds and list the clown   *laborer*
Urge on his ploughing team with cheering calls
And merry shepherds whistling toils begun
And hoarse-tongued bird-boy whose unceasing calls
Join the lark's dittys to the rising sun.

Stanzas from *Summer Images*

.   .   .

I love at early morn from new mown swath   *a row of cut grass*
To see the startled frog his rout persue
And mark while leaping o'er the dripping path
    His bright sides scatter dew
And early lark that from its bustle flys—
    To hail his matin new
    And watch him to the skies

And note on hedgerow baulks in moisture sprent   *sprinkled*
The jetty snail creep from the mossy thorn
In earnest heed and tremulous intent
    Frail brother of the morn
That from the tiny bents and misted leaves   *stalks of dry grass*
    Withdraws his timid horn
    And fearful vision weaves

And swallows heed on smoke-tanned chimney top
As wont be first unsealing morning's eye
Ere yet the bee hath gleaned one wayward drop
    Of honey on his thigh
And see him seek morn's airy couch to sing
    Until the golden sky
    Besprents his russet wing

.   .   .

And mark the evening curdle, dank and grey
Changing her watchet hue for sombre weeds   *light blue*
And moping owls to close the lids of day
    On drowsy wing proceeds
While chickering cricket tremulous and long   *chirping*
    Light's farewell inly heeds
    And gives its parting song

.   .   .

Heavy Dew

The night hath hung the morning smiles in showers,
The kingcups burnished all so rich within
Hang down their slender branches on the grass.
The bumblebees on the huge thistle flowers
Clings as half sleeping yet and motion lacks
Not even stirring as I closely pass
Save that they lift their legs above their backs
In trembling dread when touched—yet still they lie
Fearful of danger without power to fly.
The shepherd makes a mort of crooked tracks   *a lot*
His dog half-drowned and dripping to the skin
Stops oft and shakes his shaggy hide in vain
Wading through grass like rivers to the chin
Then snorts and barks and brushes on again.

Recollections after a Ramble

The rosey day was sweet & young
The clod-brown lark that haild the morn
Had just her summer anthem sung
& trembling dropped in the corn
The dew-raisd flower was perk & proud
The butterflye around it playd
The skyes blew clear save woolly cloud
That passt the sun without a shade

On the pissmires castle hill
While the burnet-buttons quakd
While beside the stone-pavd rill
Cowslip bunches nodding shakd
Bees in every peep did try   *a single blossom*
Great had been the honey shower
Soon their load was on their thigh
Yellow dust as fine as flour

Brazen magpies full of clack
Full of insolence & sport
Chattering on the donkeys back
Percht & pulld his shaggy coat
Odd crows settld on the pad   *path*
Dames from milking trotting home
Said no sign was half so bad
& shakd their heads at ills to come

While cows restless from the ground
Plungd into the stream & drank
& the rings went whirling round

Till they toucht the flaggy bank
On the arches wall I knelt
Curious as I often did
To see what the sculpture spelt
But the moss its letters hid

Labour sought the water cool
& stretching took a hearty sup
The fish were playing in the pool
& turnd their milk-white bellys up
Clothes laid down behind a bush
Wading close beside the pad
Deeply did the maiden blush
As she passd each naked lad

Some with lines the fish to catch
Quirking boys let loose from school   *searching*
Others side the hedgerow watch
Where the linnet took the wool
Tending hodge had slept too fast   *farm laborer*
While his cattle strayd abroad
Swift the freed horse gallopd past
Pattering down the stony road

The gipsey tune was loud & strong
As round the camp they danced a jig
& much I loved the brown girls song
While listning on the wooden brig   *bridge*
The shepherd he was on his rounds
The dog stopt short to lap the stream
& jingling in the fallow grounds
The ploughman urgd his reeking team

Often did I stop to gaze
On each spot once dear to me
Known mong those remembered days
Of banishd happy infancy
Often did I view the shade
Where once a nest my eyes did fill
& often markd the place I playd
At 'roly-poly' down the hill

In the woods deep shade did stand
As I passd the sticking troop
& Goody beggd a helping hand
To heave her rotten faggot up
The riding-gate sharp jerking round
Followed fast my heels again
While echo mockd the clapping sound
& 'clap clap' sung the woods amain

The wood is sweet—I love it well
In spending there my leisure hours
To seek the snail its painted shell
& look about for curious flowers
Or neath the hazels leafy thatch
On a stulp or mossy ground   *tree stump*
Little squirrels gambols watch
Oak leaves dancing round & round

Green was the shade—I love the woods
When autumns wind is mourning loud
To see the leaves float on the floods
Dead within their yellow shroud
The wood was then in glory spread

I love the browning bough to see
That litters autumns dying bed
Her latest sigh is dear to me

Neath a spreading shady oak
For awhile to muse I lay
From its grains a bough I broke
To fan the teasing flies away
Then I sought the woodland side
Cool the breeze my face did meet
& the sun the shade did hide
Tho twas hot it seemed sweet

& as while I clomb the hill
Many a distant charm I found
Pausing on the lagging mill
That scarcely movd its sails around
Hanging oer a gate or stile
Till my curious eye did tire
Leisure was employd awhile
Counting many a peeping spire

When the hot sun gan to wane
Cooling glooms fast deepning still
Refreshing greenness spread the plain
As black clouds crept the southern hill
Labour sought a sheltering place
Neath some thick wood-woven bower
While odd rain-drops dampt his face
Heralds of the coming shower

Where the oak-plank crosst the stream
Which the early-rising lass
Climbs wi milk-pail gathering cream

Crookd pads tracking thro the grass
There where willows hang their boughs
Briers & blackthorns formd a bower
Stunted thick from sheep & cows
There I stood to shun the shower

Sweet it was to feel the breeze
Blowing cool without the sun
Bumming gadflies ceasd to teaze   *buzzing*
All seemd glad the shower to shun
Sweet it was to mark the flower
Rain-drops glistning on its head
perking up beneath the bower
As if rising from the dead

& full sweet it was to look
How clouds misted oer the hill
Rain-drops how they dimpt the brook
Falling fast and faster still
While the gudgeons sturting by   *moving suddenly*
Cringd neath water-grasses shade
Startling as each nimble eye
Saw the rings the dropples made   *droplets*

& upon the dripping ground
As the shower had ceasd again
As the eye was wandering round
Trifling troubles causd a pain
Overtaken in the shower
Bumble-bees I wanderd by
Clinging to the drowking flower   *drooping*
Left without the power to fly

& full often drowning wet
Scampering beetles rac'd away

Safer shelter glad to get
Flooded out from whence they lay
While the moth for nights reprief
Waited safe & snug withall
Neath the platains bowery leaf
Where not e'en a drop could fall

Then the clouds dispers'd again
& full sweet it was to view
Sunbeams trembling long in vain
Now they 'gan to glimmer thro'
& as labour strength regains
From ales booning bounty given   *refreshing*
So revivd the freshning plains
From the smiling showers of heaven

Sweet the birds did chant their songs
Blackbird linnet lark & thrush
Music from a many tongues
Melted from each dripping bush
Deafend echo on the plain
As the sunbeams broke the cloud
Scarce could help repeat the strain
Natures anthem flowd so loud

.   .   .

Insects of mysterious birth
Sudden struck my wondering sight
Doubtless brought by moisture forth
Hid in knotts of spittle white
Backs of leaves the burthen bears
Where the sunbeams cannot stray

"Wood-sears"* called that wet declares**
So the knowing shepherds say

.   .   .

Then I stood to pause again
Retrospection sighd & smild
Musing 'tween a joy & pain
How I acted when a child
When by clearing brooks Ive been
Where the painted sky was given
Thinking if I tumbld in
I should fall direct to heaven

.   .   .

Be the journey ere so mean
passing by a cot or tree   *cottage*
In the rout theres something seen
Which the curious love to see
In each ramble tastes warm souls
More of wisdoms self can view
Than blind ignorance beholds
All lifes seven stages through

.   .   .

---

* *"wood-sears"*: cuckoo spit: 'Insects that lie in little white knots of spittle on the backs of leaves and flowers'—Clare.
** *that wet declares*: shepherds believed that wood-sears could predict the weather.

The Moors
(Sometimes called *The Enclosure*)

Far spread the moory ground, a level scene
Bespread with rush and one eternal green
That never felt the rage of blundering plough
Though centuries wreathed springs blossoms on its brow
Still meeting plains that stretched them far away
In uncheck'd shadows of green brown and grey.
Unbounded freedom ruled the wandering scene
Nor fence of ownership crept in between
To hide the prospect of the following eye.
Its only bondage was the circling sky.
One mighty flat undwarfed by bush and tree
Spread its faint shadow of immensity
And lost itself which seemed to eke its bounds
In the blue mist the (h)orison's edge surrounds.
Now this sweet vision of my boyish hours
Free as spring clouds and wild as summer flowers
Is faded all—a hope that blossomed free
And hath been once, no more shall ever be.
Enclosure came and trampled on the grave
Of labour's rights and left the poor a slave,
And memory's pride ere want to wealth did bow
Is both the shadow and the substance now.
The sheep and cows were free to range as then
Where change might prompt, nor felt the bonds of men;
Cows went and came with evening morn and night
To the wild pasture as their common right
And sheep unfolded with the rising sun
Heard the swains shout and felt their freedom won,
Tracked the red fallow field and heath and plain
Then met the brook and drank and roamed again.

The brook that dribbled on as clear as glass
Beneath the roots they hid among the grass
While the glad shepherd traced their tracks along
Free as the lark and happy as her song.
But now all's fled and flats of many a dye
That seemed to lengthen with the following eye,
Moors loosing from the sight far smooth and blea(k)
Where swooped the plover in its pleasure free,
Are vanished now with commons wild and gay
As poets' visions of life's early day.
Mulberry bushes where the boy would run
To fill his hands with fruit are grubbed and done,   *uprooted*
And hedgerow briars—flower-lovers overjoyed
Came and got flower pots—these are all destroyed,
And sky-bound moors in mangled garbs are left
Like mighty giants of their limbs bereft.
Fence now meets fence in owners' little bounds
Of field and meadow large as garden grounds,
In little parcels little minds to please
With men and flocks imprisoned, ill at ease.
Each little path that led its pleasant way
As sweet as morning leading night astray
Where little flowers bloomed round a varied host
That travel(ler) felt delighted to be lost
Nor grudged the steps that he had ta'en as vain
When right roads traced his journeys—and again
Nay on a broken tree he'd sit awhile
To see the moors and fields and meadows smile
Sometimes with cowslips smothered—then all white
With daisies—then the summer's splendid sight
Of cornfields crimson o'er the 'headach'   *common poppy*
    bloomed
Like splendid armies for the battle plumed;
He gazed upon them with wild fancy's eye

As fallen landscapes from an evening sky.
These paths are stopt—the rude philistines' thrall
Is laid upon them and destroyed them all.
Each little tyrant with his little sign
Shows where man claims earth glows no more divine,
But paths to freedom and to childhood dear
A board sticks up to notice, 'no road here',
And on the tree with ivy overhung
The hated sign by vulgar taste is hung
As though the very birds should learn to know
When they go there they must no further go.
This with the poor scared freedom bade goodbye
And much they feel it in the smothered sigh,
As birds and trees and flowers without a name
All sighed when lawless law's enclosure came,
And dreams of plunder in such rebel schemes
Have found too truly that they were but dreams.

Song's Eternity

What is songs eternity
Come and see
Can it noise and bustle be
Come and see
Praises sung or praises said
Can it be
Wait awhile and these are dead
Sigh sigh
Be they high or lowly bred
They die

What is songs eternity
Come and see

Melodys of earth and sky
Here they be
Songs once sung to adams ears
Can it be
—Ballads of six thousand years
Thrive thrive
Songs awakened with the spheres
Alive

Mighty songs that miss decay
What are they
Crowds and citys pass away
Like a day
Books are writ and books are read
What are they
Years will lay them with the dead
Sigh sigh
Trifles unto nothing wed
They die

Dreamers list the honey bee
Mark the tree
Where the blue cap tootle tee
Sings a glee
Sung to adam and to eve
Here they be
When floods covered every bough
Noahs ark
Heard that ballad singing now
Hark hark

Tootle tootle tootle tee
Can it be
Pride and fame must shadows be

Come and see
Every season own her own
Bird and bee
Sing creations music on
Natures glee
Is in every mood and tone
Eternity . . .

The eternity of song
Liveth here
Natures universal tongue
Singeth here
Songs Ive heard and felt and seen
Everywhere
Songs like the grass are evergreen
The giver
Said live and be and they have been
Forever.

III. Birds Nesting

◆◆

These closely observed bird poems are among the most impressive achievements of Clare's maturity. He intended a separate volume in which birds and their nests would be described in short poems of varying stanzas, the whole collection being called "Birds Nesting."

—Eric Robinson

Crows in Spring

The crow will tumble up and down
    At the first sight of spring
And in old trees around the town
    Brush winter from its wing

No longer flapping far away
    To naked fen they fly
Chill fare as on a winter's day
    But field and valleys nigh

Where swains are stirring out to plough
    And woods are just at hand
They seek the uplands' sunny brow
    And strut from land to land

And often flap their sooty wings
    And sturt to neighboring tree   *move suddenly*
And seems all try all ways to sing
    And almost speaks in glee

The ploughman hears and turns his head
    Above to wonder why
And there a new nest nearly made
    Proclaims the winter by

The schoolboy free from winter's frown
    That rests on every stile
In wonder sets his basket down
    To start his happy toil

Doves

Roaming the little path 'neath dotterel trees   *pollard*
Of some old hedge or spinney side, I've oft
Been startled pleasantly from musing ways
By frightened doves that suddenly aloft
Spring through the many boughs with chittering noise
Till, free from such restraints, above the head
They smacked their clapping wings for very joys.
And in a curious mood I've oft been led
To climb the twig-surrounded trunk, and there
On some few bits of sticks two white eggs lie
As left by accident, all lorn and bare
Almost without a nest; yet by and by
Two birds in golden down will leave the shells
And hiss and snap at wind-blown leaves that shake
Around their home where green seclusion dwells
Till fledged, and then the young adventurers take
The old ones timid flights from oak to oak
Listening the pleasant sutherings   *sounds of wind in the trees*
    of the shade
Nor startled by the woodman's hollow stroke
Till autumn's pleasant visions pine and fade

Then they in bolder crowds will sweep and fly
And brave the desert of a winter sky.

The Lark's Nest

From yon black clump of wheat that grows
   More rank and higher than the rest
A lark—I marked her as she rose—
   At early morning left her nest.
Her eggs were four of dusky hue
   Blotched brown as is the very ground
With tinges of a purply hue
   The larger ends encircling round.

Behind a clod how snug the nest
   Is in a horse's footing fixed!
Of twitch and stubbles roughly dressed   *couch grass*
   With roots and horsehair intermixed.
The wheat surrounds it like a bower
   And like to thatch each bowing blade
Throws off the frequent falling shower
   —And here's an egg this morning laid!

The Moor-Hen's Nest

I in my summer rambles love to see
A flood-washed bank support an aged tree
Whose roots are bare; yet some with foothold good
Crankle and spread and strike beneath the flood   *twist sinuously*
Yet still it leans as safer hold to win
On t'other side, and seems as tumbling in
Yet every summer finds it green and gay

And winter leaves it safe as did the May
Nor does the moor-hen find its safety vain
For on its roots their last year's homes remain
And once again a couple from the brood
Seek their old birthplace, and in safety's mood
Build up their flags and lay; though danger comes
It dares and tries and cannot reach their homes;
And still they hatch their eggs and sweetly dream
On their shelfed nest hung just to touch the stream;
And soon their sooty brood from fear elope
Where bulrush forests give them sweeter hope;
Their hanging nest that aids their wishes well
Each leaves for water as it leaves the shell;
They dive and dare and every gambol try
Till they themselves to other scenes can fly.

The Nightingale's Nest

Up this green woodland-ride let's softly rove
And list the nightingale—she dwells just here.
Hush! let the wood gate softly clap—for fear
The noise might drive her from her home of love;
For here I've heard her many a merry year
At morn, at eve, nay, all the livelong day
As though she lived on song. This very spot
Just where that old man's beard all wildly   *(Clematis vitalba)*
    trails
Rude arbours o'er the road and stops the way
And where that child its bluebell flowers hath got
Laughing and creeping through the mossy rails
There have I hunted like a very boy
Creeping on hands and knees through matted thorn
To find her nest and see her feed her young

And vainly did I many hours employ;
All seemed as hidden as a thought unborn.
And where those crimping fern-leaves   *rippling*
    ramp among   *luxuriate*
The hazel's under-boughs—I've nestled down
And watched her while she sung—and her renown
Hath made me marvel that so famed a bird
Should have no better dress than russet brown.
Her wings would tremble in her ecstasy
And feathers stand on end, as 'twere with joy
And mouth wide open to release her heart
Of its out-sobbing songs—The happiest part
Of summer's fame she shared—for so to me
Did happy fancies shapen her employ
But if I touched a bush or scarcely stirred
All in a moment stopt—I watched in vain:
The timid bird had left the hazel bush
And at a distance hid to sing again.
Lost in a wilderness of listening leaves
Rich ecstasy would pour its luscious strain,
Till envy spurred the emulating thrush
To start less wild and scarce inferior songs;
For while of half the year care him bereaves,
To damp the ardour of his speckled breast,
While nightingales to summer's life belongs,
And naked trees and winter's nipping wrongs
Are strangers to her music and her rest.
Her joys are evergreen, her world is wide
Hark! there she is as usual—let's be hush
For in this blackthorn clump, if rightly guessed,
Her curious house is hidden. Part aside
These hazel branches in a gentle way
And stoop right cautious 'neath the rustling boughs,
For we will have another search today

And hunt this fern-strewn thorn-clump round and round;
And where this seeded wood-grass idly bows
We'll wade right through—it is a likely nook;
In such like spots and often on the ground
They'll build, where rude boys never think to look.
Ay, as I live! her secret nest is here
Upon this whitethorn stump—I've searched about
For hours in vain—There! put that bramble by
Nay, trample on its branches and get near.
How subtle is the bird! she started out
And raised a plaintive note of danger nigh
Ere we were past the brambles; and now, near
Her nest, she sudden stops—as choking fear
That might betray her home. So even now
We'll leave it as we found it—safety's guard
Of pathless solitudes shall keep it still.
See there! she's sitting on the old oak bough
Mute in her fears; our presence doth retard
Her joys, and doubt turns every rapture chill.
Sing on, sweet bird! may no worse hap befall
Thy visions than the fear that now deceives.
We will not plunder music of its dower
Nor turn this spot of happiness to thrall
For melody seems hid in every flower
That blossoms near thy home. These harebells all
Seem bowing with the beautiful in song
And gaping orchis, with its spotted leaves
Seems blushing with the singing it has heard.
How curious is the nest! no other bird
Uses such loose materials, or weaves
Its dwelling in such spots: dead oaken leaves
Are placed without and velvet moss within
And little scraps of grass, and—scant and spare
Of what seem scarce materials—down and hair;

For from men's haunts she nothing seems to win
Yet nature is the builder, and contrives
Homes for her children's comfort even here
Where solitude's disciples spend their lives
Unseen, save when a wanderer passes near
Who loves such pleasant places. Deep adown
The nest is made, a hermit's mossy cell.
Snug lie her curious eggs in number five
Of deadened green, or rather olive-brown
And the old prickly thorn-bush guards them well.
So here we'll leave them, still unknown to wrong
As the old woodland's legacy of song.

The Pewit's Nest

Across the fallow clods at early morn
I took a random track where, scant and spare
The grass and nibbled leaves, all closely shorn
Leave a burnt flat all bleaching brown and bare
Where hungry sheep in freedom range forlorn
And 'neath the leaning willow and odd thorn
And mole-hill large that vagrant shade supplies
They batter round to shun the teasing flies
Trampling smooth places hard as cottage floors
Where the time-killing lonely shepherd boys
Whose summer homes are ever out of doors
Their chock-holes form and chalk their marble ring
And make their clay taws at the bubbling spring   *marbles*
And in their wrangling sport and gambling joys
They strime their clock-like shadows—when it cloys   *stride*
To guess the hour that slowly runs away—
And shorten sultry turmoil with their play.

Here did I roam while veering overhead
The pewit whirred in many whewing rings   *rushing, whirling*
And 'chewsit' screamed and clapped her flapping wings.
To hunt her nest my rambling step was led
O'er the broad baulk beset with little hills   *strip of grass*
By moles long formed and pismires tenanted
As likely spots—but still I searched in vain
When all at once the noisy birds were still
And on the lands a furrowed ridge between
Chance found four eggs of dingy dirty green
Deep blotched with plashy spots of chocolate stain   *wet, splashy*
Their small ends inward turned as ever found
As though some curious hand had laid them round
Yet lying on the ground with naught at all
Of soft grass, withered twitch and bleachéd weed   *couch grass*
To keep them from the rainstorms frequent fall
And here she broods on her unsavoury bed
When by and by, with little care and heed
Her young, with each a shell upon its head
Run after their wild parent's restless cry
And from their own fears tiny shadows run
'Neath clods and stones to cringe and snugly lie
Hid from all sight but the all-seeing sun
Till never-ceasing danger seemeth by.

Sand Martin

Thou hermit haunter of the lonely glen
And common wild and heath—the desolate face
Of rude waste landscapes far away from men
Where frequent quarrys give thee dwelling place
With strangest taste and labour undeterred
Drilling small holes along the quarry's side

More like the haunts of vermin than a bird
And seldom by the nesting boy descried;
I've seen thee far away from all thy tribe
Flirting about the unfrequented sky
And felt a feeling that I can't describe
Of lone seclusion and a hermit joy
To see thee circle round nor go beyond
That lone heath and its melancholy pond.

The Skylark Leaving Her Nest

Right happy bird, so full of mirth
    Mounting and mounting still more high
    To meet morn's sunshine in the sky
        Ere yet it smiles on earth

How often I delight to stand
    Listening a minute's length away
    Where summer spreads her green array
        By wheat or barley land

To see thee with a sudden start
    The green and placid herbage leave
    And in mid-air a vision weave
        For joy's delighted heart

Shedding to heaven a vagrant mirth
    When silence hushes other theme
    And woods in their dark splendour dream
        Like heaviness on earth

My mind enjoys the happy sight
    To watch thee to the clear blue sky

And when I downward turn my eye
 Earth glows with lonely light

Then nearer come thy happy sounds
 And downward drops thy little wing
 And now the valleys hear thee sing
 And all the dewy grounds

Gleam into joy! now from the eye
 Thou'rt dropping sudden as a stone
 And now thou'rt in the wheat alone
 And still the circle of the sky

And absent like a pleasure gone
 Though many come within the way
 Thy little song to peeping day
 Is still remembered on

For who that crosses fields of corn
 When skylarks start to meet the day
 But feels more pleasure on his way
 Upon a summer's morn

'Tis one of those heart-cheering sights
 In green earth's rural chronicles
 That upon every memory dwells
 Among home-fed delights

The Skylark

The rolls and harrows lie at rest beside
The battered road; and spreading far and wide
Above the russet clods, the corn is seen

Sprouting its spiry points of tender green
Where squats the hare, to terrors wide awake
Like some brown clod the harrows failed to break
Opening their golden caskets to the sun
The buttercups make schoolboys eager run
To see who shall be first to pluck the prize—
Up from their hurry, see, the skylark flies
And o'er her half-formed nest, with happy wings
Winnows the air, till in the cloud she sings
Then hangs, a dust spot in the sunny skies
And drops and drops, till in her nest she lies
Which they unheeded passed—not dreaming then
That birds which flew so high would drop again
To nests upon the ground, which anything
May come at to destroy. Had they the wing
Like such a bird, themselves would be too proud
And build on nothing but a passing cloud
As free from danger as the heavens are free
From pain and toil, there would they build and be
And sail about the world to scenes unheard
Of and unseen—Oh, were they but a bird!
So think they, while they listen to its song
And smile and fancy and so pass along
While its low nest, moist with the dews of morn
Lies safely, with the leveret, in the corn.

To the Snipe

Lover of swamps
And quagmire overgrown
With hassock-tufts of sedge, where fear encamps
Around thy home alone

The trembling grass
Quakes from the human foot
Nor bears the weight of man to let him pass
Where thou, alone and mute

Sittest at rest
In safety, near the clump
Of huge flag-forest that thy haunts invest
Or some old sallow stump

Thriving on seams
That tiny islands swell
Just hilling from the mud and rancid streams,
Suiting thy nature well

For here thy bill
Suited by wisdom good
Of rude, unseemly length, doth delve and drill
The jellied mass for food

And here, mayhap,
When summer suns have drest
The moor's rude, desolate and spongy lap
May hide thy mystic nest

Mystic indeed
For isles that oceans make
Are scarcely more secure for birds to build
Than this flag-hidden lake

Boys thread the woods
To their remotest shades
But in these marshy flats, these stagnant floods
Security pervades

From year to year
Places untrodden lie
Where man nor boy nor stock hath ventured near
Naught gazed on but the sky

And fowl that dread
The very breath of man
Hiding in spots that never knew his tread,
A wild and timid clan

Widgeon and teal
And wild duck—restless lot
That from man's dread sight will ever steal
To the most dreary spot

Here tempests howl
Around each flaggy plot
Where they who dread man's sight, the water fowl,
Hide and are frightened not

'Tis power divine
That heartens them to brave
The roughest tempest and at east recline
On marshes or the wave

Yet instinct knows
Not safety's bounds:—to shun
The firmer ground where skilking fowler goes
With searching dogs and gun

By tepid springs
Scarcely one stride across
(Though bramble from its edge a shelter flings
Thy safety is at loss)

And never choose
The little sinky foss
Streaking the moors whence spa-red water spews
From pudges fringed with moss   *puddles*

Freebooters there
Intent to kill or slay
Startle with cracking guns the trepid air
And dogs thy haunts betray

From danger's reach
Here thou art safe to roam
Far as these washy flag-sown marshes stretch
A still and quiet home

In these thy haunts
I've gleaned habitual love
From the vague world where pride and folly taunts
I muse and look above

Thy solitudes
The unbounded heaven esteems
And here my heart warms into higher moods
And dignifying dreams

I see the sky
Smile on the meanest spot
Giving to all that creep or walk or fly
A calm and cordial lot

Thine teaches me
Right feelings to employ
That in the dreariest places peace will be
A dweller and a joy

The Swallow's Nest

Here down the meadow runs a path
   Snake-winding through the pleasant hay
That leadeth over many a swath
   Which shed their fragrance all the way.
At last the eye beholds the view
   Of many arches all a-row
That leads the traveller safely through
   When floods are roaring loud below.

There 'neath an arch, as like to drop
   Two hermit swallows yearly fix
Their nest beneath the freestone top—
   You'd almost wonder how it sticks.
And through and through the brig they whip—   *bridge*
   Thoughts hardly can the pace maintain—
Then 'twit' and in the water dip,
   And 'twit' and hurry back again.

The Yellow Wagtail's Nest

Upon an eddying in a quiet nook
(We double down choice places in a book
And this I noted as a pleasant scene
Hemmed in all round with barley's juicy green)
In the thick clover-grass, at holiday
A broken plough as leisure's partner lay
A pleasant bench among the grass and flowers
For merry weeders in their dinner hours
From fallow fields released, and hot turmoil;
It nestled like a thought, forgot by toil

And seemed so picturesque a place for rest
I e'en dropped down to be a minute's guest;
And as I bent me for a flower to stoop
A little bird cheeped loud and fluttered up;
The grasses tottered with their husky seeds
That ramped beside the plough   *grew luxuriantly*
        with ranker weeds;
I looked—and there a snug nest deep and dry
Of roots and twitches entertained my eye   *couch grasses*
And six eggs sprinkled o'er with spots of grey
Lay snug as comfort's wishes ever lay.
The yellow wagtail fixed its dwelling there
Sheltered from rainfalls by the shelving share
That leaned above it like a sheltering roof
From rain and wind and tempest comfort-proof.
Such safety-places little birds will find
Far from the cares and help of human kind,
For Nature is their kind protector still
To choose their dwellings furthest off from ill;
So thought I, sitting on that broken plough
While evening's sunshine gleamed upon my brow
So soft, so sweet; and I so happy then
Felt life still Eden from the haunts of men.

The Woodlark's Nest

The woodlark rises from the coppice tree
Time after time untired she upward springs
Silent while up, then coming down she sings
A pleasant song of varied melody
Repeated often till some sudden check
The sweet-toned impulse of her rapture stops
Then stays her trembling wings and down she drops

Like to a stone among the crowding
     kecks   *the dried stalks of certain plants*
Where underneath some hazel's mossy root
Is hid her little low and humble nest.
Upon the ground larks love such places best
And here doth well her quiet station suit,
As safe as secrecy her six eggs lie
Mottled with dusky spots unseen by passers-by.

Yet chance will sometimes prove a faithless guest
Leading some wanderer by her haunts to roam
And startled by the rustle from her nest
She flutters out, and so betrays her home.
Yet this is seldom accident can meet
With her weed-hidden and surrounded nest;
I've often wondered when against my feet
She fluttered up and fanned the anemone
That blossomed round in crowds—how birds could be
So wise to find such hidden homes again.
And this in sooth oft puzzled me—they go
Far off and then return—but nature's plain:
She giveth what sufficeth them to know,
That they of comfort may their share retain.

The Wryneck's Nest

That summer bird its oft-repeated note
   Chirps from the dotterel ash, and in the hole   *pollard tree*
The green woodpecker made in years remote
   It makes its nest. When peeping idlers stroll
In anxious plundering moods, they by and by
   The wryneck's curious eggs, as white as snow
While squinting in the hollow tree, espy.

The sitting bird looks up with jetty eye
    And waves her head in terror to and fro
Speckled and veined with various shades of brown,
And then a hissing noise assails the clown.   *laborer*
    Quickly, with hasty terror in his breast
From the tree's knotty trunk he sluthers down   *slides*
    And thinks the strange bird guards a serpent's nest.

IV. *The Shepherd's Calendar:*
1823–1825

◆◆

I had a very odd dream last night and I take it as an ill omen, for I don't expect that the book will meet with a better fate. I thought I had one of the proofs of the new poems from London, and after looking at it awhile it shrank through my hands like sand, crumbling into dust.
—*from Clare's Diary, March 9, 1825*

Excerpts from *July*

Daughter of pastoral smells and sights
And sultry days and dewy nights
July resumes her yearly place
Wi' her milking maiden face
Ruddy and tann'd yet sweet to view
When everywhere's a vale of dew
And wraps it round her looks that smiles
A lovely rest to daily toils
Wi' last month's closing scenes and dins
Her sultry beaming birth begins
Hay makers still in grounds appear   *meadowlands*
And some are thinning nearly clear

.   .   .

Soon as each ground is clear of hay
The shepherd whoops his flocks away
From fallow fields to plenty scenes
Shining as smooth as bowling greens
But scared wi' clipping tides alarms   *fear of being clipped*

They bleat about the close in swarms
And hide neath hedges in the cool
Still panting tho wi'out their wool
Marked wi' the tarr'd brand's lasting dye
And make a restless hue and cry
Answering the lambs that call again
And for their old dams seek in vain
Running 'mid the stranger throng
And ever meeting wi' the wrong
Fain wi' some old ewe to abide
Who smells and tosses them aside
And some as if they knew its face
Will meet a lamb wi' mended pace
But proving hopes indulg'd in vain
They turn around and blair again *bleat*
Till wean'd from memory half forgot
They spread and feed and notice not
Save now and then to lambs' shrill cries
Odd ewes in hoarser tone replies.
Still may be seen the mowing swain
On baulks between the fields of grain *strips of grass*
Who often stops his thirst to ease
To pick the juicy pods of peas
And oft as chances bring to pass
Stoops o'er his scythe stuck in the grass
To seek the brimming honey comb
Which bees so long were toiling home
And rifl'd from so many flowers
And carried through so many hours.
He tears their small hive's mossy ball
Where the brown labourers herded all
Who gather homeward one by one
And see their nest and honey gone
Humming round his rushing toil

Their melancholy wrongs awhile
Then o'er the sweltering swaths they stray*
And hum disconsolate away.

.   .   .

The gypsy down the meadow brook
Wi' long pole and a reaping hook
Tied at its end amid the streams
That glitter wi' the hot sunbeams
Reaches and cuts the bullrush down
And hawks them round each neighboring town
Pack'd at his back or tied in loads
On asses down the dusty roads
He jogs and shouts from door to door
His well-known note of calling o'er
Offering to housewives cheap repairs
Mending their broken-bottomed chairs
Wi' step half-walk half-dance, and eye
Ready to smile on passers-by

.   .   .

The gypsy fiddler jogs away
To village feast and holiday
Scraping in public house to try
What beer his music will supply
From clowns who happy wi' the din   *yokels*
Dance their hand-nail'd hilos thin.   *heavy boots*
Along the roads in passing crowds
Followed by dust like smoking clouds
Scotch droves of beast, a little breed
In sweltered weary mood proceed,
A patient race from scottish hills

*swaths: a row of cut grass as it falls from the scythe

To fatten by our pasture rills
Lean wi' the wants of mountain soil
But short and stout for travel's toil
Wi' cocked-up horns and curling crown
And dewlap bosom hanging down
Followed by slowly pacing swains
Wild to our rushy flats and plains
At whom the shepherd's dog will rise
And shake himself and in surprise
Draw back and waffle in affright   *whimper, yelp*
Barking the traveller out of sight
And mowers o'er their scythes will bear
Upon their uncouth dress to stare
And shepherds as they trample by
Leaves o'er their hooks a wondering eye
To witness men so oddly clad
In petticoats of banded plaid
Wi' blankets o'er their shoulders slung
To camp at night the fields among
When they for rest on commons stop
And blue cap like a stocking top
Cock't o'er their faces summer-brown
Wi' scarlet tassels on the crown
Rude patterns of the thistle flower
Untricked and open to the shower
And honest faces fresh and free
That breathe of mountain liberty.

.   .   .

Soon as the morning wakens red
The shepherd startles from his bed
And rocks afield his moving pace
Till folded sheep will know his face
Rising as he appears in sight

To shake their coats as in delight
His shadow stalking stride for stride
Stretches a giant by his side
Long as a tree without a top
And oft it urges him to stop
Both in his journey and his song
And wonders why it seems so long
And by and by as morning dies
Shrinks to an unbritch'd boy in size
Then as the evening gathers blue
Grows to a giant's length anew
Puzzled the more he stops to pause
His wisdom vainly seeks the cause.
Again his journey he pursues
Lengthening his track along the dews
And his dog that turn'd to pick
From his sides the sucking tick
Insects that on cattle creep
And bites the labourer laid asleep
Pricks up his ears to see t'was gone
And shakes his hide and hastens on
And the while the shepherd stay'd
Trailing a track the hare had made
Bolts through the creeping hedge again
And hurrying follows wi' the swain
The singing shouting herding boys
Follows again their wild employs.

.   .   .

The breeze is stop't, the lazy bough
Hath not a leaf that dances now
The totter grass upon the hill   *quaking grass*
And spiders' threads is hanging still
The feathers drop't from moore-hen's wings

Upon the water's surface clings
As steadfast and as heavy seem
As stones beneath them in the stream
Hawkweed and groundsels fairy downs
Unruffl'd keep their seeding crowns
And in the oven-heated air
Not one light thing is floating there
Save that to the earnest eye
The restless heat swims twittering by.
The swine run restless down the street
Anxious some pond or ditch to meet
From day's hot swoonings to retire
Wallowing in the weeds and mire.
The linnets seek the twigs that lie
Close to the brook and brig stones dry   *bridge*
At top and sit and dip their bills
Till they have drunk their little fills
Then flirt their wings and wet their feathers
To cool them in the blazing weathers
Dashing the water o'er their heads
Then hie them to some cooling sheds
Where dark wood glooms about the plain
To prick their feathers smooth again.
The young quick's branches seem as dead
And scorch from yellow into red
Ere autumn hath its pencil ta'en
Their shades in different hues to stain.

.   .   .

How sweet the village evening comes
To weary hinds from toil released   *farm laborers*
And panting sheep and tortured beast
The shepherd long wi' heat opprest
Betakes him to his cottage rest

And his tired dog that plods along
Wi' panting breath and lolling tongue
Runs eager as the brook appears
And dashes in head over ears
Startling reed sparrow broods to fly
That in the reed woods slumber'd nigh
And water ratts in haste to hide
Nibbling the sedges close beside
Lapping while he floats about
To quench his thirst then drabbles   *emerges bedraggled, muddy*
  out
And shakes his coat and like the swain
Is happy night is come again.

. . .

The black house bee hath ceas'd to sing
And white nosed one wi'out a sting
That boys will catch devoid of dread
Are in their little holes abed
And martins 'neath the mossy eves
Oft startl'd at the sparrow thieves
That in their house will often peep
Breaking their little weary sleep
And oft succeed when left alone
In making their clay huts their own
Where the cock sparrow on the scout
Watches and keeps the owners out.
The geese have left their home-close moats
And at the yard gate clean their coats
Or 'neath their feathers tuck their heads
Asleep till driven to their sheds
The pigeon droves in whisking flight
Hurrying to their cotes ere night
In coveys round the village meet

And in the dove cote holes retreat;
Nor more about the wheaten grounds
The bird boy's bell and clapper sounds
Retiring wi' the setting sun
His toil and shout and song is done.
The shrill bat wi' its flitting mate
Starts through the church vault's iron gate.
Death's daily visitors and all
He meets save slanting suns that fall
At eve as if they lov'd to shed
Their daily memory o'er the dead.

.   .   .

V. Northborough: Near Madness, 1832–1837

❖❖

In heaven, too,
You'd be institutionalized.
But that's all right,—
If they let you eat and swear
With the likes of Blake,
And Christopher Smart,
And that sweet man, John Clare.
——Theodore Roethke

Stanzas from *The Flitting*

I've left my own old home of homes
Green fields and every pleasant place
The summer like a stranger comes
I pause and hardly know her face
I miss the hazel's happy green
The bluebells' quiet hanging blooms
Where envy's sneer was never seen
Where staring malice never comes

I miss the heath, its yellow furze
Molehills and rabbit tracks that lead
Through beesom ling and teazel burrs   *broom* and *heather*
That spread a wilderness indeed
The woodland oaks and all below

That their white-powdered branches shield
The mossy pads—the very crow   *paths*
Croaked music in my native fields

   .   .   .

I dwell on trifles like a child
I feel as ill becomes a man
And still my thoughts like weedlings wild
Grow up to blossom where they can
They turn to places known so long
And feel that joy was dwelling there
So homebred pleasure fills the song
That has no present joys to heir

   .   .   .

Strange scenes mere shadows are to me
Vague unpersonifying things
I love with my old haunts to be
By quiet woods and gravel springs
Where little pebbles wear as smooth
As hermit's beads by gentle floods
Whose noises doth my spirits soothe
And warms them into singing moods

   .   .   .

I love the verse that mild and bland
Breathes of green fields and open sky
I love the muse that in her hand
Bears wreaths of native poesy
Who walks nor skips the pasture brook
In scorn—but by the drinking horse
Leans o'er its little brig to look   *bridge*
How far the sallows lean across   *willows*

. . .

I love the muse who sits her down
Upon the molehill's little lap
Who feals no fear to stain her gown
And pauses by the hedgerow gap
Not with that affectation praise
Of song to sing and never see
A field flower grow in all her days
Or e'en a forest's ancient tree

E'en here my simple feelings nurse
A love for every simple weed
And e'en this little 'shepherd's purse'   *a common weed*
Grieves me to cut it up—Indeed
I feel at times a love and joy
For every weed and every thing
A feeling kindred from a boy
A feeling brought with every spring

And why—this 'shepherd's purse' that grows
In this strange spot in days gone by
Grew in the little garden rows
Of that old hut now left—and I
Feel what I never felt before
This weed an ancient neighbour here
And though I own the spot no more
Its every trifle makes it dear

The ivy at the parlour end
The woodbine at the garden gate
Are all and each affection's friend
That renders parting desolate
But times will change and friends must part

And nature still can make amends
Their memory lingers round the heart
Like life whose essence is its friends

Time looks on pomp with careless moods
Or killing apathy's disdain
—So where old marble cities stood
Poor persecuted weeds remain
She feels a love for little things
That very few can feel beside
And still the grass eternal springs
Where castles stood and grandeur died

November

The shepherds almost wonder where they dwell
And the old dog for his night journey stares
The path leads somewhere but they cannot tell
And neighbor meets with neighbor unawares
The maiden passes close beside her cow
And wanders on and thinks her far away
The ploughman goes unseen behind his plough
And seems to loose his horses half the day
The lazy mist creeps on in journey slow
The maidens shout and wonder where they go
So dull and dark are the November days
The lazy mist high up the evening curled
And now the morn quite hides in smoky haze
The place we occupy seems all the world

Autumn Birds

The wild duck startles like a sudden thought
And heron slow as if it might be caught
The flopping crows on weary wing go by
And greybeard jackdaws noising as they fly
The crowds of starnels whizz and hurry by
And darken like a cloud the evening sky
The larks like thunder rise and suther   *make a sighing noise*
    round
Then drop and nestle in the stubble ground
The wild swan hurries high and noises loud
With white necks peering to the evening cloud
The weary rooks to distant woods are gone
With length of tail the magpie winnows on
To neighboring tree, and leaves the distant crow
While small birds nestle in the hedge below

Rook's Nest

The rooks begin to build, and pleasant looks
The homestead elms now almost black with rooks
The birds at first for mastership will try
They fight for sticks and squabble as they fly
And if a stranger comes they soon invade
And pull his nest to pieces soon as made
The carrion crow and hawk dare never come
They dare to fight like armies round their home
The boughs will hardly bear their noisy guests
And storms will come and overturn their nests
They build above the reach of clauming clowns   *clutching*
They climb and fast but cunning cuts them down

Others with reaching poles the nest destroys
While off and up they fly with deafening noise

The Partridge

One day across the fields I chanced to pass
When chickens chelped and skuttled in the grass   *chirped*
And as I looked about to find the seat
A wounded partridge dropped against my feet.
She fluttered round and calling as she lay
The chickens chelped and fluttered all away.
I stooped to pick her up when up she drew
Her wounded wing and cackled as she flew.
I wondered much to hear the chickens lie
As still as nothing till I wandered by
And soon she came again with much ado
And swept the grass and called them as she flew
But still they kept their seat and left no trace
And old cows snorted when they passed the place.

The Tramp

He eats (a moment's stoppage to his song)
The stolen turnip as he goes along;
And hops along and heeds with careless eye
The passing crowded stage-coach reeling by.
He talks to none, but wends his silent way,
Or under any hedge his house is made.
He has no calling and he owns no trade.
An old smoked blanket arches o'er his head,
A wisp of straw or stubble makes his bed.
He knows a lawless law that claims no kin

But meet and plunder on and feel no sin—
No matter where they go or where they dwell,
They dally with the winds and laugh at hell.

The Puddock's Nest   (The kite: *Milvus milvus*)

The sailing puddock sweeps about for prey
And keeps above the woods from day to day
They make a nest so large in woods remote
Would fill a woman's apron with the
     sprotes   *twigs for firewood*
And schoolboys daring doing tasks the best
Will often climb and stand upon the nest
They find a huge old tree and free from snags
And make a flat nest lined with wool and rags
And almost big enough to make a bed
And lay three eggs and spotted o'er with red
The schoolboy often hears the old ones* cry
And climbs the tree and gets them ere they fly
And takes them home and often cuts their wing
And ties them in the garden with a string

The Gipsy Camp

The snow falls deep; the Forest lies alone:
The boy goes hasty for his load of brakes,   *brushwood*
Then thinks upon the fire and hurries back;
The Gipsy knocks his hands and tucks them up,
And seeks his squalid camp, half hid in snow,
Beneath the oak, which breaks away the wind,

*a slip: Clare meant "young ones"

And bushes close, with snow-like hovel warm:
There stinking mutton roasts upon the coals,
And the half-roasted dog squats close and rubs,
Then feels the heat too strong and goes aloof;
He watches well, but none a bit can spare,
And vainly waits the morsel thrown away:
'Tis thus they live—a picture to the place,
A quiet, pilfering, unprotected race.

(Written at High Beach Asylum, in 1840 or early 1841)

VI. Northampton: Madness, 1841–1864

❖❖

> Say maiden wilt thou go with me
> Through this sad non-identity
> Where parents live and are forgot
> And sisters live and know us not . . .
>
> This land of shadows wilt thou trace
> And look—nor know each other's face
> The present mixed with reasons gone
> And past, and present all as one . . .
> —from "An Invite to Eternity"

> Born to misfortunes—where no sheltering bay
> Keeps off the tempest—wrecked where'er I flee
> I struggle with my fate—in trouble strong—
> Mary thy name long loved still keeps me free
> Till my lost life becomes a part of thee
> —from "Child Harold"

Stanzas from *Child Harold*

1) Many are poets—though they use no pen
   To show their labours to the shuffling age
   Real poets must be truly honest men
   Tied to no mongrel laws on flattery's page
   No zeal have they for wrong or party rage
   —The life of labour is a rural song

That hurts no cause—nor warfare tries to wage
Toil like the brook in music wears along—
Great little minds claim right to act the wrong

2) My life hath been one love—no blot it out
   My life hath been one chain of contradictions
   Madhouses, Prisons, whore shops—never doubt
   But that my life hath had some strong convictions
   That such was wrong—religion makes restrictions
   I would have followed—but life turned a bubble
   And clumb the giant stile of maledictions
   They took me from my wife and to save trouble
   I wed again and made the error double

3) How servile is the task to please alone
   Though beauty woo and love inspire the song
   Mere painted beauty with her heart of stone
   Thinks the world worships while she flaunts along
   The flower of sunshine, butterfly of song
   Give me the truth of heart in woman's life
   The love to cherish one—and do no wrong
   To none—O peace of every care and strife
   Is true love in an estimable wife

4) How beautiful this hill of fern swells on
   So beautiful the chapel peeps between
   The hornbeams—with its simple bell—alone
   I wander here hid in a palace green
   Mary is absent—but the forest queen
   Nature is with me—morning noon and gloaming
   I write my poems in these paths unseen
   And when among these brakes and beeches roaming
   I sigh for truth and home and love and woman

5)   I have had many loves—and seek no more
     These solitudes my last delights shall be
     The leaf-hid forest—and the lonely shore
     Seem to my mind like beings that are free
     Yet would I had some eye to smile on me
     Some heart where I could make a happy home in
     Sweet Susan that was wont my love to be
     And Bessy of the glen—for I've been roaming
     With both at morn and noon and dusky gloaming

6)   Cares gather round, I snap their chains in two
     And smile in agony and laugh in tears
     Like playing with a deadly serpent—who
     Stings to the death—there is no room for fears
     Where death would bring me happiness—his sheers
     Kills cares that hiss to poison many a vein
     The thought to be extinct my fate endears
     Pale death the grand physician cures all pain
     The dead rest well—who lived for joys in vain

7)   Life is to me a dream that never wakes
     Night finds me on this lengthening road alone
     Love is to me a thought that ever aches
     A frost-bound thought that freezes life to stone
     Mary in truth and nature still my own
     That warms the winter of my aching breast
     Thy name is joy nor will I life bemoan—
     Midnight when sleep takes charge of nature's rest
     Finds me awake and friendless—not distres't

8)   Tie all my cares up in thy arms O sleep
     And give my weary spirits peace and rest
     I'm not an outlaw in this midnight deep

If prayers are offered from sweet woman's breast
One and one only made my being blest
And fancy shapes her form in every dell
On that sweet bosom I've had hours of rest
Though now through years of absence doomed to dwell
Day seems my night and night seems blackest hell

9)   Fame blazed upon me like a comet's glare
     Fame waned and left me like a fallen star
     Because I told the evil what they are
     And truth and falsehood never wished to mar
     My Life hath been a wreck—and I've gone far
     For peace and truth—and hope—for home and rest
     —Like Eden's gates—fate throws a constant bar—
     Thoughts may o'ertake the sunset in the west
     —Man meets no home within a woman's breast

10) Though they are blazoned in the poet's song
     As all the comforts which our lives contain
     I read and sought such joys my whole life long
     And found the best of poets sung in vain
     But still I read and sighed and sued agin
     And lost no purpose where I had the will
     I almost worshiped when my toils grew vain
     Finding no antidote my pains to kill
     I sigh a poet and a lover still

(Begun at High Beach Asylum in 1841, continued at Northborough, and completed at Northampton.)

Song

I hid my love when young while I
Couldn't bear the buzzing of a fly
I hid my love to my despite
Till I could not bear to look at light
I dare not gaze upon her face
But left her memory in each place
Where e're I saw a wild flower lie
I kissed and bade my love good bye

I met her in the greenest dells
Where dew drops pearl the wood blue bells
The lost breeze kissed her bright blue eye
The Bee kissed and went singing by
A sun beam found a passage there
A gold chain round her neck so fair
As secret as the wild bees' song
She lay there all the summer long

I hid my love in field and town
Till e'en the breeze would knock me down
The Bees seemed singing ballads o'er
The flys' buzz turned a Lion's roar
And even silence found a tongue
To haunt me all the summer long
The Riddle nature could not prove
Was nothing else but secret love

Song

Love lives beyond
The tomb—the earth—which fades like dew
I love the fond
The faithful and the true

Love lives in sleep
The happiness of healthy dreams
Eve's dews may weep
But love delightful seems

Tis seen in flowers
And in the even's pearly dew
On earth's green hours
And in the heaven's eternal blue

Tis heard in spring
When light and sunbeams warm and kind
On angel's wing
Bring love and music to the mind

And where is voice
So young and beautifully sweet
As nature's choice
When spring and lovers meet

Love lives beyond
The tomb the earth the flowers and dew
I love the fond
The faithful young and true

Written in Prison

I envy e'en the fly its gleams of joy
In the green woods from being but a boy
Among the vulgar and the lowly bred
I envied e'en the hare her grassy bed
Inured to strife and hardship from a child
I traced with lonely step the desert wild
Sigh'd o'er bird pleasures but no nest destroyed
With pleasure felt the singing they enjoyed
Saw nature smile on all and shed no tears
A slave through ages though a child in years
The mockery and scorn of those more old
An Aesop in the world's extended fold
The fly I envy settling in the sun
On the green leaf and wish my goal was won

The Yellowhammer

When shall I see the white thorn leaves again
And Yellowhammers gath'ring the dry bents   *old dry grass*
By the Dyke side on stilly moor or fen
Feathered with love and nature's good intents
Rude is the nest this Architect invents
Rural the place with cart ruts by dyke side
Dead grass, horse hair and downy-headed bents
Tied to dead thistles she doth well provide
Close to a hill o' ants where cowslips bloom
And shed o'er meadows far their sweet perfume
In early Spring when winds blow chilly cold
The yellowhammer trailing grass will come
To fix a place and choose an early home
With yellow breast and head of solid gold

Evening

How beautiful the eve comes in
The grazing kine the village din
Of happy children, cocks and hens
And chickens cheeping in their pens
And hogs that grunt the roots to eat
And dogs asleep on their fore-feet
And sparrows on the mossy thatch
Waiting whatever they may catch
Beneath the oak the old cart shed
There the capon goes to bed
On the old crippled wagon-sea(t)
Propped up with an axle-tree
By the wall on broken rail
Tweets red-breasted firetail
And their neighbour's pied flycatch(er)
Build cobweb nest in the old thatch
Where beesom weed—that high wind   *heath* or *broom*
    leaves
Blossoms and blooms above the eaves
The old cow-crib is mossed and green
As if it just had painted been
The ramping kecks in orchard gaps   *cow parsley*
Shake like green neighbours in white caps
On which the snail will climb and dwell
For three weeks in its painted shell
There the white-nosed 'clock a clay'   *ladybird*
Red and black spotted sits all day
Round which the white-nosed bee will hum
To which the black-nosed bee will come
More than a hundred times a day
Till evening shadows cool in grey

Wormwood, burdock—the cart conceals
Rotting and wanting both the wheels
The battered wagon wanting three
Stands prop't with broken axle-tree
A hen pen with two slats away
A hen and chickens gone astray
A barrow left without a wheel
Since spring, which nettles now conceal
From free stones getting on the moor
The creeping donkeys pass the door
The geese on dunghills clean their quills
And squabble o'er the dainty pills   *peels*
Thrown out by the housewife's cares
Who supper for her man prepares
Labour returning from its toils
Ditcher that the earth besoils
Hedgers from the wattled thorn
Scaring birdboy with his horn
Who blows it to the wandering moon
And thinks the village knows the tune
The shepherd in the nearly dark
Followed by his dog's gruff bark
The milkmaid tripping through the dew
Singing all the evening through
The owlet through the barn hole peeps
And all the village hides and sleeps.

First Love

I ne'er was struck before that hour
   With love so sudden and so sweet
Her face it bloomed like a sweet flower
   And stole my heart away complete

My face turned pale a deadly pale
    My legs refused to walk away
And when she looked what could I ail
My life and all seemed turned to clay

And then my blood rushed to my face
    And took my eyesight quite away
The trees and bushes round the place
    Seemed midnight at noon day
I could not see a single thing
    Words from my eyes did start
They spoke as chords do from the string
    And blood burnt round my heart

Are flowers the winter's choice
    Is love's bed always snow
She seemed to hear my silent voice
    Not love's appeals to know
I never saw so sweet a face
    As that I stood before
My heart has left its dwelling place
    And can return no more—

An Invite to Eternity

Wilt thou go with me sweet maid
Say maiden wilt thou go with me
Through the valley depths of shade
Of night and dark obscurity
Where the path hath lost its way
Where the sun forgets the day
Where there's nor life nor light to see
Sweet maiden wilt thou go with me

Where stones will turn to flooding streams
Where plains will rise like ocean waves
Where life will fade like visioned dreams
And mountains darken into caves
Say maiden wilt thou go with me
Through this sad nonidentity
Where parents live and are forgot
And sisters live and know us not

Say maiden wilt thou go with me
In this strange death of life to be
To live in death and be the same
Without this life, or home, or name
At once to be and not to be
That was, and is not—yet to see
Things pass like shadows—and the sky
Above, below, around us lie

The land of shadows wilt thou trace
And look—nor know each others face
The present mixed with reasons gone
And past, and present all as one
Say maiden can thy life be led
To join the living with the dead
Then trace thy footsteps on with me
We're wed to one eternity

Stanzas

Black absence hides upon the past
    I quite forget thy face
And memory like the angry blast
    Will love's last smile erace

I try to think of what has been
  But all is blank to me
And other faces pass between
  My early love and thee

I try to trace thy memory now
  And only find thy name
Those inky lashes on thy brow
  Black hair, and eyes the same
Thy round pale face of snowy dyes
  There's nothing paints thee there
A darkness comes before my eyes
  For nothing seems so fair

I knew thy name so sweet and young
  'Twas music to my ears
A silent word upon my tongue
  A hidden thought for years
Dark hair and lashes swarthy too
  Arched on thy forehead pale
All else is vanished from my view
  Like voices on the gale.

Lord Hear My Prayer*

Lord hear my prayer when trouble glooms
Let sorrow find a way
And when the day of trouble comes
Turn not thy face away
My bones like hearth stones burn away
My life like vapoury smoke decays

*from the 102nd Psalm: 1–17

My heart is smitten like the grass
That withered lies and dead
And I so lost to what I was
Forget to eat my bread
My voice is groaning all the day
My bones prick through the skin of clay

The wilderness'es pelican
The desert's lonely owl
I am their like a desert man
In ways as lone & foul
As sparrows on the cottage top
I wait till I with faintness drop

I bear my enemies reproach
All silently I mourn
They on my private peace encroach
Against me they are sworn
Ashes as bread my trouble shares
& mix my food with weeping cares

Yet not for them is sorrow's toil
I fear no mortal's frown
But thou hast held me up awhile
& thou hast cast me down
My days like shadows waste from view
I mourn like withered grass in dew

But thou Lord shall endure forever
All generations through
Thou shalt to Zion be the giver
Of joy & mercy too
Her very stones are in their trust
Thy servants reverence her dust

Heathens shall hear and fear thy name
All kings of earth thy glory know
When thou shalt build up Zion's fame
& live in glory there below
He'll not despise their prayers though mute
But still regard the destitute

I Am

I am—yet what I am, none cares or knows;
   My friends forsake me like a memory lost:
I am the self-consumer of my woes;
   They rise and vanish in oblivion's host,
Like shadows in love's frenzied stifled throes:
And yet I am, and live—like vapours toss't

Into the nothingness of scorn and noise—
   Into the living sea of waking dreams,
Where there is neither sense of life or joys,
   But the vast shipwreck of my life's esteems;
Even the dearest, that I love the best
Are strange—nay, rather, stranger than the rest.

I long for scenes where man hath never trod
   A place where woman never smiled or wept
There to abide with my Creator, God,
   And sleep as I in childhood sweetly slept,
Untroubling, and untroubled where I lie,
The grass below—above the vaulted sky.

To Mary

I sleep with thee, and wake with thee,
And yet thou art not there:—
I fill my arms, with thoughts of thee,
And press the common air.—
Thy eyes are gazing upon mine,
When thou art out of sight;
My lips are always touching thine,
At morning, noon and night.

I think, and speak of other things
To keep my mind at rest:
But still to thee, my memory clings,
Like love in womans breast;—
I hide it from the worlds wide eye;
And think, and speak contrary;
But soft, the wind comes from the sky,
And wispers tales of Mary.—

The night wind wispers in my ear,
The moon shines in my face;
A burden still of chilling fear,
I find in every place.—
The breeze is wispering in the bush;
And the dew-fall from the tree,
All: sighing on, and will not hush,
Some pleasant tales of thee.—

A Vision

I lost the love of heaven above;
I spurned the lust of earth below;
I felt the sweets of fancied love,
And hell itself my only foe.

I lost earth's joys but felt the glow
Of heaven's flame abound in me;
Till loveliness and I did grow
The bard of immortality.

I loved but woman fell away;
I hid me from her faded fame:
I snatched the sun's eternal ray
And wrote till earth was but a name.

In every language upon earth,
On every shore, o'er every sea,
I gave my name immortal birth
And kept my spirit with the free.

Sources

❖❖

1. Editions of Clare's Poetry and Prose

Poems Descriptive of Rural Life and Scenery. Printed for Taylor and Hussey, and E. Drury. London 1820. 2nd edition 1920.

John Clare: Poems Chiefly from Manuscript. Edited by Edmund Blunden and Alan Porter. Cobden-Sanderson. London 1920.

Sketches in the Life of John Clare by Himself. With an Introduction by Edmund Blunden. Cobden-Sanderson. London 1931.

The Poems of John Clare (2 vols). Edited by J. W. and Anne Tibble. Dent. London 1935.

Poems of John Clare's Madness. Edited by Geoffrey Grigson. Routledge & Kegan Paul. London 1949.

A Selection of Poetry and Prose. Edited by Edmund Blunden. Rupert Hart-Davis. London 1950.

Selected Poems of John Clare. Edited by Geoffrey Grigson. Routledge & Kegan Paul. London 1950.

The Letters of John Clare. Edited by J. W. and Anne Tibble. Routledge & Kegan Paul. London 1950.

The Prose of John Clare. Edited by J. W. and Anne Tibble. Routledge & Kegan Paul. London 1951.

Selected Poems of John Clare. Edited and with an Introduction by James Reeves. Heinemann. London 1954.

The Later Poems of John Clare. Edited with an Introduction by Eric Robinson and Geoffrey Summerfield. Manchester University Press. 1964.

The Shepherd's Calendar. Edited with an Introduction by Eric Robinson and Geoffrey Summerfield. Oxford University Press. 1964.

Clare: Selected Poems and Prose. Edited by Eric Robinson and Geoffrey Summerfield. Oxford University Press. 1966.

John Clare: Selected Poems. Edited with an Introduction by Elaine Feinstein. University Tutorial Press. London 1968.

Birds Nest. Edited by Anne Tibble. MidNAG. Northumberland 1973.

John Clare: The Midsummer Cushion. Edited by Anne Tibble and R. K. R. Thornton. MidNAG/Carcanet Press. Manchester 1978.

John Clare: Bird Poems. Edited by Peter Levi. The Folio Society. 1980.

The Autobiographical Writings of John Clare. Edited by Eric Robinson. Oxford University Press. 1983.

The Natural History Prose Writings of John Clare. Edited by Margaret Grainger. Clarendon Press. Oxford 1983.

John Clare (The Oxford Authors Series). Edited by Eric Robinson and David Powell. Oxford University Press. 1984.

The Later Poems of John Clare (2 vols). Edited by Eric Robinson and David Powell. Clarendon Press. Oxford 1984.

The Parish, a Satire, by John Clare. Edited by Eric Robinson. Viking. New York 1985.

John Clare: Selected Poetry and Prose. Edited by M. and R. Williams. Methuen English Texts. London & New York 1986.

The Early Poems of John Clare (2 vols). Edited by Eric Robinson and David Powell. Clarendon Press. Oxford 1989.

2. Biography and Criticism

John Clare: A Life. J. W. and Anne Tibble. Cobden-Sanderson. 1932.

Green Shadows: A Life of John Clare. June Wilson. Hodder & Stoughton. London 1951.

John Clare: His Life and Poetry. J. W. and Anne Tibble. Heinemann. London 1956.

John Clare: A Life. J. W. and Anne Tibble. Michael Joseph. London 1972.

The Idea of Landscape and the Sense of Place in the Poetry of John Clare. J. D. Barrell. Cambridge University Press. 1972.

The Poetry of John Clare: A Critical Introduction. Mark Storey. Routledge & Kegan Paul. London 1973.

In Adam's Garden: A Study of John Clare's Pre-asylum Poetry. Janet M. Todd. University of Florida Press. 1973.

John Clare. (Twayne's English Authors Series). William Howard. Twayne. 1981.

A Right to Song: The Life of John Clare. Edward Storey. Metheun. London 1982.

John Clare and the Bounds of Circumstance. Johanne Clare. McGill–Queen's University Press. 1987.

3. General

The Rural Muse. Rayner Unwin. George Allen and Unwin. London 1954.

The Making of English Landscape. W. G. Hoskins. Hodder & Stoughton. London 1955.

The Crowning Privilege (pp. 53–62). Robert Graves. Doubleday. New York 1956.

A Visit to Mrs Wilcox (pp. 56–66). Naomi Lewis. Cresset Press. London 1957.

The Lyric Impulse. C. Day Lewis. Chatto and Windus. London 1965.

The Country and the City. Raymond Williams. Chatto and Windus. London 1973.

About the Editor

Carolyn Kizer has published five books of poetry, including Mermaids in the Basement, The Nearness of You, *and* YIN, *which won the Pulitzer Prize in 1985. She is noted for her translations from the Chinese and is the author of* Carrying Over: Poems from the Chinese, Urdu, Macedonian, Yiddish, and French African.